iDentities

PAUL SELIGSON and **ALASTAIR LANE**

Richmond

WORKBOOK 1

Contents

Unit 1 ....Page 3

Unit 2 ....Page 8

Unit 3 ....Page 13

Unit 4 ....Page 18

Unit 5 ....Page 23

Unit 6 ....Page 28

Unit 7 ....Page 33

Unit 8 ....Page 38

Unit 9 ....Page 43

Unit 10 ....Page 48

Unit 11 ....Page 53

Unit 12 ....Page 58

Selected audio scripts ....Page 63

Answer key ....Page 67

1 » 1.1 What's the story behind your name?

A Answer Amir's riddles about members of his family.

1. I have a cousin, Sam. Sam's wife's mother is Sam's _____.
2. Zubeida, my lovely _____, is my husband's child from his first marriage.
3. My _____ is 101! He's my dad's granddad.
4. I don't have any (half) brothers or sisters, so that makes me an _____.
5. My sister and I are _____. I call her my little sister though, because she's two minutes younger than me!
6. My father's grandfather's great grandson is my _____.

B Complete the missing family words in Suzie's blog.

Suzie's space

family | friends | music | films

Let me tell you about my family. We're not, perhaps, what you would expect! My mom became a (1) s_____ mom because she got divorced when I was a kid. Then she met Gary and remarried. Gary, my (2) s_____ is great, and they have a baby now. So suddenly we're a family of four: me, mom, Gary and my (3) h_____-b_____, Nathan. Gary was an (4) o_____ child and he has a very close relationship with his dad. Unfortunately my mom doesn't get along with her new (5) f_____-i_____-l_____ at all! I hope that'll change soon!

C ▶1 Use five of these verbs in the correct form to complete conversations 1–5. Listen to check.

| bring up | get along | look after | look up | make up | run in |

1. A: Is your family very competitive?
   B: We sure are, especially my brother and me. We had a huge argument over a basketball game last weekend, but we _____ again afterwards!
2. A: Athletic success _____ your family, doesn't it?
   B: Yeah, especially on my dad's side. He was a professional skier. My grandma was a professional skier, too. And now I'm one.
3. A: Does everyone _____ well in your family?
   B: Yes, well, except for my two grandfathers. They don't like each other at all!
4. A: Is there anyone that you really _____ to in your family?
   B: Yes, my grandma. She had eight kids! Can you imagine that? She was amazing.
5. A: How often do you have to _____ your younger brother and sister?
   B: Not often. They're both in their teens now so they don't need adult supervision in the evening.

D Write true answers to two of A's questions in **C**.

1. _____
2. _____

1.2 Do / Did you get along with your parents?

A Read the online forum. Check (✓) the problems you had (or have) with your parents.

B Replace the bold *get* verbs with these verbs in the correct form. One is used twice.

> arrive at   become   have an opportunity
> receive   understand

 What annoys you about your parents?

 When I'm in the bathroom for ten minutes or more, they **get** angry and start banging on the door.   1 _____

 My parents are always criticizing my look. It's like, why are you wearing jeans and that T-shirt? They just don't **get** me.   2 _____

 I never **get** to watch what I want on TV. My dad's always in the living room, watching sports programs.   3 _____

 If I don't **get to** the table in time for meals, they start calling me on my phone. "Where are you?" It drives me crazy.   4 _____

 When I was a kid, all my friends **got** an allowance, but did I? No! Never. I had to wash the car or look after my baby brother just to get $5.   5 _____

 My mom **gets** really mad when I don't clean my room. But I don't see why. After all it's mine, not hers!   6 _____

C Order the words in 1–6 to make sentences.

1 asking / not / help / bad / idea / is / for / a

2 on / but / we / started / carried / tennis / raining / playing / it

3 it's / to / on / not / going / exhibit / Sunday / the / worth

4 baby / new / a / having / exhausting / is / totally

5 help / about / nervous / next week's / can't / feeling / I / exams

6 ideas / new / thinking / for / a / of / hard / time / have / I / work

D Make it personal Rewrite two sentences in B so they're true for you.

1 _____
2 _____
3 _____

How many pets have you lived with? 1.3

A Read the blog post and check (✓) its main purpose.
1 To offer advice for pet owners.
2 To make people laugh.
3 To complain about the author's pet.

B Re-read and match underlined phrases 1–3 with definitions a–e. There are two extra ones.

a ☐ a lot   b ☑ ever   c ☐ mostly
d ☐ in reality   e ☐ anywhere

IS YOUR CAT PLOTTING TO KILL YOU?

Don't get me wrong. I love pets. I wouldn't hurt an animal ¹ <u>in a million years</u>. The thing is, would they say the same about us? When your kitty is lying in front of the radiator in a state of complete happiness, is she dreaming of being a tiger in the jungle, hunting wildlife … or hunting you?

How to tell if your cat is plotting to kill you? is the subject of a book and an online feed, and it is the funniest site ² <u>on earth</u>. Owners take pictures of their pet when it clearly has murder in mind. Notice that look of annoyance on your cat's face? Oh yes, watch out!

The book is extremely funny, and I've started looking at my cat, Cloud, with new eyes. If she's plotting to kill me, what would she do if my hamster escaped in the living room? Cloud would be ³ <u>a thousand times</u> more dangerous to a little orange thing like that. One false move and my hamster would quickly see its Facebook® status change from "pet" to "snack." I'm starting to think that perhaps it's only our size that keeps us alive.

C ▶2 Complete what these pet owners said with a form of the word in CAPITALS. Listen to check.
1 Pet _____ownership_____ isn't easy, but it's a wonderful experience. OWNER
2 I love cats because they're so _____. AFFECTION
3 I think almost everyone in this _____ has a dog. NEIGHBOR
4 We didn't know anything about keeping a pet iguana, but the salesperson at the pet shop was very _____ and explained everything to us. HELP
5 The countryside is the best place to have a horse because you have the _____ to ride wherever you want. FREE
6 Ricky taught his parrot to speak, and now it's incredibly _____. It doesn't shut up! TALK
7 We've lost the tortoise! It's Cathy's fault. She's always so _____. This time, she left it alone in the garden, and now it's disappeared! CARE
8 Having a dog has brought us so much _____. I can't imagine life without our furry friend. HAPPY

D Make it personal Complete this sentence so it's true for you.

In my opinion, _____ make perfect pets because _____
_____.

1.4 What difficult people do you know?

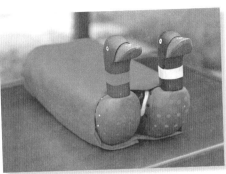

A ▶3 Listen and number Ki-Yeon's problems in the order you hear them, 1–4. One problem isn't mentioned.

Ki-Yeon's ...
- ☐ aunt is calling him a lot.
- ☐ cousin can't come to the wedding.
- ☐ family doesn't want to pay for the wedding.
- ☐ fiancée can't find a wedding dress.
- ☐ brother hasn't taken care of the invitations yet.

B ▶3 Listen again. T (true) or F (false)?
1. In Korea, it's traditional to give wooden ducks as a wedding present.
2. Ki-Yeon doesn't like his mother-in-law.
3. In Korea, the grandparents pay half the cost of the wedding.
4. The wedding ceremony is in February.
5. Ki-Yeon's cousin is expecting a baby.
6. Ki-Yeon talked to his aunt about the food for the wedding.

C Complete the wedding advice using the words in parentheses.

What are your tips for organizing a wedding?

1. _It's essential for you to tell_ everyone what time the ceremony begins. (essential / you / tell)

2. _____ your guests the details over the phone. (better / not / give)

3. _____ each guest a map of how to get to the wedding. (advisable / send)

4. _____ stressed, but you should try not to panic. (hard / not / get)

5. _____ all your guests to respond to the wedding invitations. (good / idea / you / ask)

6. _____ the food before you know exactly how many people are coming. (no / point / choose)

D Make it personal What's your best piece of advice for a close friend who's getting married next week?

_____
_____

Do you still make voice calls? 1.5

Writing an effective paragraph

A Complete the paragraph with these connectors.

> besides   it's important   lastly
> on top of that   to begin with

Smart phones: a curse for all generations?

Many parents give their kids a smartphone as a form of babysitter, even during family meals. However, (1) _____ for parents to think carefully before allowing their children to bring a smartphone to the dinner table. (2) _____ , this suggests that it's fine for children to use their gadgets on social occasions. (3) _____ , it prevents shy children from learning how to interact with other family members and makes it difficult for older relatives to begin a conversation with them. (4) _____ , many games on these devices are incredibly addictive, and children play them too much already. (5) _____ , dinner is a moment for a family to enjoy quality time together. Smartphones disrupt that happy atmosphere.

> HONEY, COULD YOU TEXT THE KIDS AND TELL THEM THAT DINNER IS READY?

B Choose the best topic sentence (a–c) to complete three paragraphs from other student essays.

(1) ☐ Teenagers are so glued to their smartphones that they lose interest in talking to other family members. Sometimes they are so engaged with the screen that they don't even say hello to their parents when they get home from work.

a Teenagers spend too much time playing games online.
b Some parents are unable to communicate clearly with their kids.
c Using technology makes teenagers antisocial.

(2) ☐ People can receive work emails or messages at the dinner table, in the bathroom, or even as they are getting ready for bed. This can increase stress levels at home when they should be trying to relax.

a The biggest problem is the number of instant messages that people send and get about unimportant things.
b It is no use thinking that someone's job stops when he or she leaves the office.
c People spend too long on the computer in the office.

(3) ☐ Children and younger teens often stay glued to their devices late into the night. This makes them tired and even angry the next day, and that causes arguments. Some educators suggest that it is essential for parents to turn the house WiFi off at night. But is that a solution? Children can still access the Internet on their phones.

a Many problems come from not getting enough sleep.
b Parents are worried about the cost of all this technology.
c The problems are worse in the evening than the morning.

C Write a new topic sentence for a paragraph in **B**, using your own ideas.

_____

_____

D Look back at lessons 1.1–1.5 in the Student's Book. Find the connection between the song lines and the content of each lesson.

E ▶4 Listen to the five question titles from the unit, and record your answers to them. If possible, compare recordings with a classmate.

7

2 » 2.1 What's most on your mind right now?

A Do the crossword. Read the clues and make noun modifiers.

ACROSS

1 I flew from London to Japan last week. The nine-hour time difference really messed up my body _____ .

4 The main social _____ in our country are poverty, unemployment, and homelessness.

5 Dad was in a car _____ . Another car hit him on the highway but luckily, no one was hurt.

6 The adolescent _____ is different from the adult one, so teenagers think differently from older people.

7 The patient was suffering from stress, which disturbed her sleep _____ . She kept waking up in the middle of the night.

DOWN

2 Finding _____ activities you like is the best way to deal with stress. I do Zumba, a mix of dance and aerobics from Colombia.

3 We always have a big family _____ at lunchtime on Sundays, cooked by my oldest sister.

4 I find it hard to make an _____ decision. I need time to think before I say "yes" or "no".

7 _____ pressure is one of the biggest problems in high school. You feel like you have to do the same things as your friends.

B Complete 1–5 with one word each from box A and box B. Each box has one extra word.

A family financial material physical romantic scientific	**B** appearance dynamics fact possessions problems relationships

1 Someone who finds it difficult to talk to people and make friends may have difficulty in forming _____ .

2 _____ occur when you spend more than you earn on a regular basis.

3 Many philosophers feel that _____ such as cars, homes, and expensive clothes are not important for true happiness.

4 _____ should not be a factor in whether a job applicant gets a job or not. It is your skills that are important, not how you look.

5 A _____ is something that is clearly true and cannot be disputed by other experts. It isn't an opinion or a theory.

C Correct the mistake in each sentence.

1 I keep worry about my flight next week. What if it gets canceled? _____

2 I think to my grandma night and day. She's been in the hospital for months. _____

3 I can't seem making any progress with my college project. It's impossible. _____

4 I can't stop to think about my operation next week. I don't want to have it! _____

5 I consider leaving my job because I'm so unhappy at my company. _____

D **Make it personal** Rewrite two sentences in C so they're true for you.

1 _____

2 _____

Do you worry about your diet? 2.2 «

A Read the interview. Replace the bold words with these phrases. There are two extras.

> a big deal   at a disadvantage   wears off
> keep you going   treat   a waste of time
> wears off   weight gain   in an accident with

Ask the expert

What should triathletes eat and drink?

Miranda Blanco, triathlete

Not sugar! Sugar gives you a big energy boost, but it soon **disappears**. If you eat lots of sugar, it may also explain **a sudden increase in kilos**. If you want chocolate or candy, eat it as a **special favor to yourself**, not a main part of your diet.

1 _____
2 _____
3 _____

Water doesn't give you energy, but if you get dehydrated your performance will suffer. When competing in sports events, remember to drink lots of water or you'll be **in a worse position** to the other athletes.

4 _____

Getting enough iron is **very important** in maintaining a healthy diet, especially for women. Good sources of iron are cereals and green vegetables like spinach.

5 _____

Pasta is the super food for any athlete, especially whole wheat pasta. This releases energy slowly, so it will **give you energy** throughout your event.

6 _____

B ▶5 Complete Miranda's comments 1–5 with one word in each blank. Listen to check.

1 The problem _____ going on a diet is that you always feel hungry.
2 The best _____ about the swimming pool is the sauna. It's the perfect place to relax.
3 One disadvantage _____ running is that it can damage your knees if you do it over a long period.
4 The good thing about _____ rice before exercise is that it gives you lots of energy.
5 The worst thing about training for the competition _____ getting up early in the morning.

C Read the article and circle the correct alternatives.

The pros and cons of eating fruit, fruit, and nothing but fruit!

In the world of weird diets, fruitarianism is the most extreme of all. Fruitarians only eat fruit, no vegetables, and nothing cooked. The best thing about the diet is [1]*that / what* people discover exotic fruit from around the world, like durian (pictured). The [2]*worse / worst* thing about the diet is [3]*can place / it can place* people in the hospital.

The biggest disadvantage of fruitarianism is [4]*this / that* the diet doesn't include essential food groups like fat or protein. [5]*This is / These are* necessary for a healthy body. Another disadvantage [6]*of / to* the diet is that fruitarians don't drink coffee or eat chocolate, which [7]*is / are* both extremely hard to give up.

Nevertheless, people can and do choose the fruitarian route. The easiest part of [8]*be / being* a fruitarian is the first few days when the body feels different – but this is only a temporary change.

The hardest part is [9]*keep / keeping* the diet up. That should come as no surprise. The problem [10]*about / with* fruitarianism is that our bodies are not designed for a fruit-only diet, which means that there are serious health risks for its followers. It is not a long-term option for good health.

9

>> 2.3   Who's the most intelligent person you know?

A Which do you think is more important in life: being intelligent or looking intelligent?
Read the article to check if the author shares your opinion.

How to look more intelligent in 6 easy steps

Jervis Jameson

There is lots of advice out there on how to be more intelligent, but the truth of the matter is that appearance is more important than reality. It's better just to look more intelligent … and anyone's capable 1_____ looking like Einstein, without making any special effort.

1   Dress the part. When shown a photo of a woman in smart clothes and the same woman in casual wear, most people thought the first woman was more intelligent than the second one. It's amazing, but if you wear a suit to work like me, people assume you are good 2_____ your job.

2   A double negative makes a positive, e.g. "I don't dislike your work." People find it difficult 3_____ follow double negatives, and they think people who use them are more clever than others.

3   According to psychologists, people think that if someone looks them in the eye during conversation, they assume the person is highly intelligent.

4   Researchers at the University of Melbourne believe they have found a link between intelligence and people who wear glasses. It seems that eyeglass wearers really are more adept 4_____ doing complicated tasks. Now if I could just find mine in the mornings …

5   It's all in the voice. If you're skilled 5_____ speaking slowly and clearly, people will believe you know what you are talking about. Talking loudly is a big no-no.

6   Never tell people you're intelligent. If you have a gift 6_____ something like math or programming, keep it under your hat. Really smart people tend to be modest in their everyday lives.

B Complete the phrases 1–6 in the article.

C Re-read and check (✓) the statements we can infer about the author.

1 Jervis Jameson believes that people can train themselves to be more intelligent. ☐

2 He's a very lazy person. ☐

3 He often wears very formal clothes. ☐

4 He's extremely serious. ☐

5 He's quite forgetful. ☐

6 He talks very loudly in his everyday life. ☐

D Complete 1–6 with a reference word.

1 I asked two people in the store to help me. The first ignored me, and the _____ refused to help me because she was on her break!

2 You can tell what kind of photo you have by _____ filename: .gif or .jpeg, for example.

3 In college, I discovered the theory of multiple intelligences, _____ completely changed how I judge the success of my students.

4 Not one student had brought a pen with _____ . They were so unprepared for my lessons!

5 There are so many people that I follow on Twitter®, but there's only _____ that always makes me laugh.

6 Harry was the person _____ intelligence test put him in the top 2% of people in the country.

Do you enjoy science fiction? 2.4

A 🔊6 Listen to a discussion about the *chupacabra* ('the goat-sucker'). Who thinks it might exist (✓)? Who doesn't believe it exists (✗)?

Frank Mortimer ☐   Rachel Schultz ☐   Alba Lopez ☐

B 🔊6 Listen again. Correct the wrong information in 1–4.

1 It all began in March 1995 in Puerto Rico. A farmer discovered eight goats with all their blood missing. _____

2 Eyewitnesses say that the chupacabra is gray with brown eyes. It moves like a kangaroo, and it has spines on its back. _____

3 There have been reports of chupacabras in Puerto Rico, the continental United States, Argentina, and Chile. _____

4 The coyote might have been ill. When they're ill, coyotes can become tired and gray, like descriptions of the chupacabra. _____

C Circle the correct alternatives in the comments on the *Science Fiction or Science Fact?* website.

Science Fiction or Science Fact?

1 The farmer *must / can't* have seen something strange on that night in 1995.

2 People invent stories like this all the time because they *might just want / just have wanted* to get their photo in the paper.

3 It can't *be / have been* a monster that killed those eight animals on that night. It's science fiction!

4 An animal like the chupacabra *may exist / have existed* somewhere in Puerto Rico. They're discovering new species all the time.

D 🔊7 Complete 1–5 with the correct form of the verbs. Listen to check.

1 A: Pete didn't reply to my email yesterday.
   B: He might not _____ (see) it.

2 A: I saw Kim over the weekend, but I didn't have time to speak to her.
   B: What? It can't _____ (be) Kim. She was in Chicago!

3 A: Jim's lost his coat. He can't find it anywhere.
   B: He may _____ (leave) it in the cafeteria. He had it when we ate lunch.

4 A: Look at this. The bank says I have $2,000 in my account, but I didn't put it there.
   B: Someone at the bank must _____ (make) a mistake.

5 A: Did it rain last night? The laundry isn't dry.
   B: It couldn't _____ (rain). Look, the ground isn't wet.

2.5 What was the last test you took?

A for-and-against essay

A Complete the essay with these connectors.

> a further advantage   a number of drawbacks   one advantage of
> on the one hand   on the other hand   to sum up   ~~while~~

Modern students are being tested to death. Discuss.

Teachers and parents are worried that students are taking too many tests. Some students take a test after every unit of their coursebook [1] _____*while*_____ others have frequent exams throughout the year.

[2]_____ frequent tests is that they show what students really know. Today all the knowledge in the world is one click away. In a test, students must show clear understanding of their subject. [3]_____ is that tests motivate students to study.

However, there are [4]_____ to frequent testing. Tests take up a lot of class time that could normally be better spent teaching. Tests are also demotivating for weaker students. Furthermore, the purpose of these tests is not always clear, for example, just to give teachers a quiet class. [5]_____, tests are an opportunity to spot which students are struggling and to see where review is necessary.

[6]_____, these tests might actually be simply to prove that schools are teaching the approved syllabus set by the government. In other words, the tests may not actually be for the benefit of the individual students at all.

[7]_____, students are taking too many tests, and these are occupying class time that could be better used in other ways. Tests should only be given when there is a clear need for them, for example, as a final exam. Other forms of evaluation can be much fairer and more productive.

B Decide if 1–4 are F (for) or A (against) the title "Modern students are being tested to death."

1 Tests for ten-year-olds may only be a simple test of their ability, whereas many ten-year-olds feel under enormous pressure to pass them.

2 One further drawback is that the more tests there are, the less time there is for fluency practice in language classes, as it is not practical to give speaking tests to 40 or more students each week.

3 Although it can be argued that students take too many tests today, schools in my country actually tested students more in the past than they do today.

4 One further advantage of testing is that it prevents cheating. Students cannot simply cut and paste an answer that they have "Googled".

C Write your own conclusion to the for-and-against essay question in **A**.

To sum up, _____

_____ .

D Look back at lessons 2.1–2.5 in the Student's Book. Find the connection between the song lines and the content of each lesson.

E ▶8 Listen to the five question titles from the unit, and record your answers to them. If possible, compare recordings with a classmate.

3 » 3.1 Do you get embarrassed easily?

A Do the verb puzzle. Then choose the correct picture a–d for 8 (the word in gray).

1. To open your mouth, usually wide, because you're tired, sometimes with a rude noise!
2. To open a door by moving it away from you.
3. To fall because you accidentally hit something with your foot.
4. To look at something for a long time without looking away. It rhymes with *hair*, *pear*, and *square*.
5. The opposite of clue 2. It rhymes with *full* and *wool*.
6. To look at something quickly for a short time, then look away. It rhymes with *dance*.
7. To express emotion or pain with a long, loud, high sound. It rhymes with *seem* and *dream*.

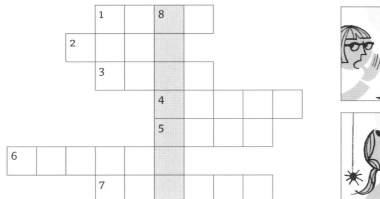
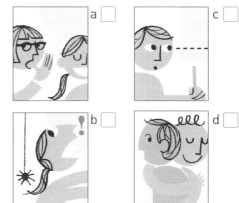

B Cross out the incorrect choice for each sentence.

1. The official *glanced / pushed / stared* at my passport photo when I arrived at the airport.
2. A lady *screamed / whispered / yawned* my name, but I'd never seen her before.
3. A tall man *glanced / tripped / pushed* me when I was trying to get on the bus.
4. We *pushed / pulled / screamed* the dog out of the car.
5. The lion *stared / whispered / yawned* while I took its photo.

C ◯9 Complete the conversation with these words. There's one extra. Listen to check.

| believe | but | happens | go | know | then | thing |

A: Did I tell you about my work trip last week?
B: No, ¹_____ on. Continue.
A: Three colleagues and I are traveling to a conference with our boss. He's going to drive, so he tells us to meet him in the parking lot. But when we get there, it's full of cars, and we aren't sure where he is.
B: So what ²_____ next?
A: I call him and I say "We're in the parking lot next to this really old red car that looks like a maniac has been driving it". Before I ³_____ it, everyone's staring at me.
B: And ⁴_____ what?
A: I just keep talking. I say, "Yeah, yeah, the car has these bumps and scratches and a really stupid 'Dog on board' sign in the back window." You won't ⁵_____ what happens next. My boss says "That's my car."
B: Oh no!
A: The next ⁶_____ I know, the car door opens and my boss gets out. He looks absolutely furious. He doesn't talk to me all the way to the meeting – and it's a four-hour trip! I just wanted to die!

13

3.2 How often do you take selfies?

A Read the article and circle the correct alternatives.

"There are selfies and there are selfies"

Japanese astronaut Aki Hoshide ¹*traveled / was traveling* on the International Space Station when he ²*took / had taken* the selfie of the year. Hoshide ³*had worked / was working* outside the Space Station when he ⁴*captured / had captured* his perfect snap.

If you look carefully in his helmet, you will see what made this photo so special. Hoshide ⁵*had waited / had been waiting* second after second for the perfect moment when the earth and the space station both ⁶*appeared / had appeared* in a straight line. In the instant when the earth ⁷*arrived / was arriving* at the right spot, Hoshide ⁸*hit / had been hitting* the button. After he ⁹ *was putting / had put* the picture on the Internet, Twitter ¹⁰*went / had gone* crazy. There are already almost 3,000 retweets of the selfie from space. Beat that, Ellen DeGeneres!

B ▶ 10 Complete 1–6 with the correct form of the verbs. Listen to check.

1 I took an amazing selfie while I _____ (walk) around Washington D.C. In it, you can see me standing on Pennsylvania Avenue, with a great view of the White House behind me. Gorgeous!
2 I was on a boat and I was about to take a photo of a whale when I _____ (drop) my camera in the water! And it would have been the best picture ever! What a shame!
3 It was only when I looked at my camera and saw some terrible photos that I realized my six-year-old son _____ (take) photos with it.
4 My favorite childhood photo was taken when my parents, my brother, and I _____ (camp) in the woods. The expression on my face shows how happy I was.
5 We saw Novak Djokovic, the tennis player, but I couldn't take a photo because I _____ (leave) my camera at home.
6 Someone took a photo of me while I _____ (watch) a baseball game, and it ended up in the newspaper!

C Make it personal What's the best selfie you've ever taken? Use 1–3 from **B** as a model to help you.

_____
_____

What invention can't you live without? 3.3

A Read the blog below about hot new inventions and check (✓) the correct options in the chart.

	The author likes it	The author doesn't like it	The author gives no opinion
1 Ice cream			
2 Toasting knife			
3 PEG			

B From the context, guess the meaning of the bold words in the blog. Match them to definitions 1–8.

1 cut into thin parts, as we do with meat, cheese, or pizza _____
2 people who don't eat any animal products _____
3 an expression meaning *something is my responsibility* _____
4 expensive _____
5 a long thin object that can be metal or wood – nature, it's part of a tree _____
6 useful _____
7 appears when you don't expect it _____
8 visible when there's no light _____

Innovations round-up
Katerina Oblov

Summer's here, and we're all feeling a little bit lazy over at HQ. Nevertheless, now and again a fun new gadget still **pops up** on our Facebook page. **It's up to me** to let you know what's out there. Here are July's top-three innovations:

1 We've just discovered something that is completely different – **glow-in-the-dark** ice cream. It comes in several different flavors, including raspberry, and its light comes from a natural food flavoring. Not being made with any dairy products, it's suitable for **vegans** and people who cannot drink milk.

2 The handheld toasting knife is out of this world. I've never seen anything like it before. The knife heats up and toasts bread while you **slice** it. It makes perfect toast time after time. It's my pick of the month.

3 In our office, we've been arguing a lot about PEGs (personal energy generators). Basically, a PEG is a **stick** that you carry, and while you move, walk, or run it generates energy. You then use it as an emergency battery. Basically, people who are into adventure sports like hiking think it's really **handy**. Sooner or later the battery always runs out though, usually when you're miles and miles away from anywhere. I'm more of an indoor person and I'm not eager to buy the PEG that I saw, especially because at $200 each, it's pretty **pricey**.

C Complete 1–6 with binomials.

1 My parents have been married for fifty years. They've had their ups and _____ like any couple, but they still love each other enormously.
2 What do you think are the pros and _____ of taking early retirement?
3 Diana put her heart and _____ into writing that book, so she was so disappointed when it never got published.
4 I'm afraid this is the apartment we've rented, so for better or _____, we're now stuck with it.
5 I was walking along a beach in Cancún when I suddenly came face to _____ with my boss!
6 We've told him over and _____ not to forget to recharge his laptop, but he never listens!

» 3.4 What was your favorite activity as a child?

A ▶11 Listen to a conversation about childhood fads. Complete 1–6 with *Ron* or *Mary*.

1 _____ got into the fad at the age of 12.
2 _____ always used to eat the same thing while doing the activity.
3 _____ used to do the fad in the 1980s.
4 _____ started the fad after receiving a birthday present.
5 _____ stopped the fad while still at school.
6 _____ wants to do the fad again in the future.

B ▶11 Listen again. T (true) or F (false)?

1 Ron used to dress up in special clothes when playing role-playing games.
2 Ron used to play the games in the dining room.
3 Ron plays the games with his children.
4 Mary used to go roller-blading with her friends and her family.
5 Mary's roller-blades were lots of different colors.
6 Mary doesn't have any roller-blades now.

C Correct the mistake in each extract.

1 When I was twelve, my mom used to buy me a surfboard. We lived next to the beach, and I would go surfing every weekend. _____
2 I used to play basketball every week. We used to win the State Championship once in 2009. _____
3 When I was a kid, I would to collect comics. I would go to the local comic-book shop once a week, and I'd buy loads of different ones. _____
4 I wasn't use to have any hobbies when I was a kid. The educational system in my country was very strict, and we used to have a lot of extra classes in the evenings. _____

D Make it personal Complete the sentences so they're true for you.

1 As a child, I used to _____ after school, and then I would _____ or _____ .
2 A few years ago, I didn't use to _____ , but now I do it all the time.
3 When I was a bit younger, I used to _____ a lot, and once I _____ .

What makes you really happy? 3.5

Telling a story (1)

A ▶12 Read the story and circle the correct alternatives. Listen to check.

Last month I was at my college library because I wanted to use the computers. I put my flash drive into the machine ¹*as / initially* I logged on and waited. ²*Eventually / Initially*, nothing happened, so I waited, but the PC wouldn't recognize my flash drive. ³*All of a sudden / Some time later*, I decided to restart the computer. It took ages to restart so ⁴*finally / in the meantime*, I started sending some WhatsApp® messages on my smartphone. As I was tapping on my phone, the girl next to me was looking at me angrily. I didn't know why so I ignored her. ⁵*Eventually / At first*, the computer started up again, but it still wouldn't recognize my flash drive. I was starting to get really annoyed because it still wasn't working, so I put the flash drive in and out again several times. ⁶*All of a sudden / As*, the girl next to me leaned over, looking like she wanted to speak to me. ⁷*Finally / In the meantime* she said, "Could you please stop trying to put your flash drive into my computer!"

B Replace the bold words in each sentence with a synonym.
1 I nervously opened the letter from the government. **At first**, I thought I owed money, but in the end, I realized that they were actually paying me. Yeah! _____
2 The water went off **just as** I was having a shower. My hair was full of shampoo, and we didn't have any more water for the rest of the day! _____
3 I made the sandwiches for our son's party. **Meanwhile**, my wife made the cake. _____
4 I tried calling the office for hours, but nobody replied. **In the end**, I realized that it was five o'clock in the morning in their country! _____
5 We were having coffee when **all of a sudden** Billy screamed. There was a huge spider under the table! _____
6 I was chatting with this guy because I thought he was a new student in our class. **Some time later**, I discovered that he was our new teacher! _____

C Correct the mistake in each extract.
1 I was walking down the street in L.A. last month when all of a suddenly, I saw Jennifer Lawrence! _____
2 I put this video online and forgot about it. Well, some time late, I discovered that it had gone viral in Canada. It was amazing. _____
3 Jim did the ironing. In the meanwhile, I cleaned the bathroom. _____
4 I almost had an accident on my bike. I was riding down the street, and there was a tree in the road. I didn't see initially it, but luckily, I stopped in time. _____
5 We spent ages trying to buy tickets for the concert online, but after while, we just gave up. It was impossible. _____

D Look back at lessons 3.1–3.5 in the Student's Book. Find the connection between the song lines and the content of each lesson.

E ▶13 Listen to the five question titles from the unit, and record your answers to them. If possible, compare recordings with a classmate.

4 » 4.1 Are you ever deceived by ads?

A Read the story and circle the correct alternatives.

Spider in ear is a web of lies

You've all seen the video. A man has a pain in his ear. He goes into the bathroom. He can't figure ¹*out / over* what is causing his discomfort until he reaches over the sink and – gross! – discovers that a spider is living in his ear.

All the online media outlets were completely taken ²*in / off* and ran the story along with the video. Unfortunately, it turned ³*in / out* to be a hoax!

So how come all these journalists and editors fell ⁴*for / off* the trick once again? It's because this was not a video made by a teenager in his bedroom, but the work of Bruce Branit, a special effects professional.

Branit knew what people watch ⁵*away / out* for when they try to spot a fake. Great images and special effects often give ⁶*away / over* the fact that the video is a fake. Instead, Branit used a simple iPhone® and made the image shaky, so it looked amateur. Only an expert can tell a fake and a real video ⁷*off / apart*.

The image of the spider in the ear may seem unbelievable … because that's exactly what it is!

B ▶ 14 Put the words in italics in order to complete the conversation. Listen to check.

A: Look at this video! It shows an eagle attacking a man in a park.

B: Come on! *that / surely / agree / you'll* ¹_____ it's a fake.

A: It's on a real news website.

B: Just because it's on a newspaper's website *mean / authentic / it's / doesn't* ²_____ .

A: I tell you it must be real. *way / it / look / at / this* ³_____ . How could they train an eagle to do that?

B: *point / missing / the / you're* ⁴_____ ! None of this is real. There is no eagle. They can make a bird using special effects. A kid can do that on a computer.

A: You're just a cynic.

B: *me / way / another / it / let / put* ⁵_____ . How could they be filming at the exact moment when the eagle attacked? It's almost impossible.

A: That's why it went viral – because it's a unique video!

B: Honestly, you'll believe anything. You should go and work for one of those websites.

C **Make it personal** Complete the sentences so they're true for you.

1 The last online video I fell for was _____ .

2 What gives me away when I get embarrassed is _____ .

3 The last time I bought something that turned out to be a complete waste of money was _____ .

18

Are teachers important in the digital age? 4.2

A Read the blog about Keele University in the U.K. True (T) or False (F)?

1 All courses at Keele are taught face to face.

2 The blog author found the equipment difficult to use at first.

3 KAVE prepares students better than traditional teaching methods.

B Complete the blog with these conjunctions.

despite   even though   in spite   unlike   whereas

The anatomy of the classroom of the future

¹_____ I had chosen to study Anatomy, I was still feeling nervous when I began my course at Keele University in the UK. ²_____ my friends who were studying history and languages, I was on an intense, challenging science course. They were studying books, ³_____ I was studying the human body.

So I was delighted on my first day to discover KAVE (the Keele Active Virtual Environment). It's a virtual reality program for students like me.

To use KAVE, I was given special glasses and a special stick, which was used to zoom in and out on things I was seeing. ⁴_____ of the fact that it was my first time in a virtual classroom like this, I soon got the hang of it, and I became absorbed in my work. I used it to travel around a hospital as if I were a doctor.

It is amazingly realistic. The system has been a great success for almost everyone who has tried it. ⁵_____ not having the same amount of physical contact with patients and illness, students who used KAVE consistently got better grades at the end of the course. It is the classroom of the future, today!

C Match 1–5 to a–f to make sentences. There is one extra ending.

1 Schools today have interactive whiteboards unlike

2 Although my teacher is not a native speaker of English,

3 In spite of practicing it for hours with my teacher,

4 We learned a lot of English in school despite

5 TV programs in Spain are usually dubbed into Spanish

a ☐ I still can't pronounce the rolled 'r' in Spanish!

b ☐ while those in Turkey are in the original language with subtitles.

c ☐ mine, which had a blackboard and a piece of chalk!

d ☐ to have no coursebooks at all.

e ☐ the fact that we had classes with 50 students!

f ☐ she's one of the best I have ever had.

D Make it personal Complete the sentences so they're true for you.

1 Even though I've been learning English for quite a while, _____.

2 Despite having read a lot in English _____.

3 Unlike listening in my own language, listening in English _____.

4 In spite of my accent in English, _____.

4.3 What was the last rumor you heard?

A Read and complete the urban legend with questions a–f. There's one extra.

a Where does this urban legend come from?
b How did criminals find out about it?
c Why did the banks never introduce this system?
d What is the ATM hoax?
e Are there any other problematic PINs?
f What happens when you do that?

Urban legend of the week: the ATM Hoax

This week, we're talking to Sally Redmond about one of the most famous tricks of recent times, the ATM hoax.

Q: ¹ _____

Back in the day, people said that if someone tried to steal money from you at an ATM, you should enter your PIN number backwards.

Q: ² _____

It's like an instruction. This tells the bank that someone is trying to rob you. It sounds an alarm, and the police should arrive **in no time**.

Q: ³ _____

It all started in a 1980s news article that discussed this idea as a suggestion from a bank. In fact, the suggestion was never adopted, so the news article is out-of-date. And today? **At first** someone must have come across the original story and written about it on Facebook. Then it went viral through Twitter. And it re-appears **from time to time**.

Q: ⁴ _____

It doesn't work. **In the end**, they abandoned the idea because they realized that lots of people have a PIN that reads the same backwards and forwards, like 2552.

Q: ⁵ _____

How about one like 1131? **At some point**, a user is going to hit the wrong key and enter 1311 by mistake. Are the police going to come running every time that happens? This whole story is just an urban legend, nothing more.

B Replace the underlined words with the bold phrases in **A**.

1 I tried to dissolve a tooth in soda when one fell out. <u>After a long time</u>, nothing happened. _____
2 They told me that Taylor Swift was going to play a secret gig in my city. <u>In the beginning</u>, I believed them, but I soon realized it was just a rumor. _____
3 <u>A long time ago</u>, people said that if you ate carrots, it improved your eyesight – and actually it's true. They contain vitamin A, which is essential for good vision. _____
4 If you talk about the moon landing, <u>there will always be a moment when</u> someone will say it's a hoax and it never happened. Get real, people! _____
5 <u>Occasionally</u> you read these stories in the paper about someone finding a frog or an insect in a bag of salad in the supermarket. They gross me out! _____
6 You often hear stories about people finding something horrible in a burger in the fast-food restaurant, and <u>almost immediately</u> it's all over the Internet. It's hard to tell if these stories are true or false. _____

C ▶15 Complete 1–6 with these phrases. Listen to check.

| a bird | a broken record | cats and dogs | a glove | wildfire | the wind |

1 A: The doctors struggle to control this disease.
   B: I know. It's unstoppable. It spreads like _____.

2 A: You didn't really get along with your sister, did you?
   B: Not at all. We fought like _____ when we were little.

3 A: Your horse is fast, isn't she?
   B: You're telling me! She runs like _____.

4 A: This bus is always full of people! I hate it!
   B: You say that every time we get on it. Honestly, you sound like _____.

5 A: How was the dress? Did you try it on?
   B: It's like it was made for me. It fits like _____.

6 A: Kaitlin is looking really thin these days. I'm really worried about her.
   B: Yes, she does a lot of exercise, but she eats like _____.

How would you describe yourself? 4.4

A ▶16 Listen to the podcast on look-alikes: people who look the same. T (true) or F (false)?

1 Both speakers know someone who looks like them.
2 Most people have about two look-alikes in the world.
3 They recommend using the Internet to find a look-alike.

B ▶16 Listen again. Check (✓) the correct answers.

1 How did Luisa, the presenter, meet her look-alike?
   a ☐ At a party.
   b ☐ By chance.
   c ☐ They're relatives.
2 What do we know about her appearance?
   a ☐ She's tall.
   b ☐ She wears glasses.
   c ☐ She has brown eyes.
3 Why does Jacques believe we all have a look-alike?
   a ☐ Because he personally knows a lot of people with a look-alike.
   b ☐ Because there are very few facial shapes.
   c ☐ Because there are so many people in the world.
4 Why do they mention the Mongol emperor Genghis Khan?
   a ☐ He is the ancestor of many people alive today.
   b ☐ He had a twin brother who looked like him.
   c ☐ He had over 200 look-alikes.
5 What do they say about TwinStrangers.net?
   a ☐ It's free.
   b ☐ It uses illustrations.
   c ☐ It doesn't have many users.

Genghis Khan

C ▶16 Circle the correct option to complete the sentences. Listen again to check.

1 There was a woman next to me who was travelling *by / with* herself.
2 My husband said "You two look like *every / each* other."
3 That's natural, but we're talking about strangers who look like one *other / another*.
4 We like to have a very special image of *ourselves / us*.
5 You choose drawings that describe *you / yourself*.

D Complete 1–10 with one word in each gap.

1 My cousin and I look a lot like _____ other. People often think we're sisters!
2 Nobody wanted to go to Sicily with Jack, so he went by _____ .
3 I have five brothers and sisters. It's great. We all help one _____ around the house.
4 When I compared my photo with one of my granddad at the same age, I even surprised _____ . We look identical!
5 Actors like me are all the same. We don't like watching _____ when we're on TV or film.
6 Don't worry. Just be _____ at the interview.
7 Pete and Sara only talked to each _____ at the party.
8 That's the new head of marketing. Let's go over and introduce _____ .
9 I made some great friends at school. We've all kept in touch with one _____ since we left.
10 My aunt Rosie has lived by _____ since her husband passed away.

4.5 How many pairs of glasses do you own?

A Read the review quickly. How many stars is it (1–5)?

Adrift with the Oculus Rift ☆☆☆☆☆

a _____

The future of gaming has arrived with the Oculus Rift virtual reality headset. ¹For the m_ _t p_r_, when people think of virtual reality, they think of terrible graphics in 90s movies. You can forget that – with these goggles, you'll enter a new world of exploration.

b _____

Although the number of possible applications is endless, ²on av_ _ _g_, most people will use them for gaming. The games available are standard ones like soccer, and it is like you're in the stadium on the field.

c _____

When playing games, you use hand-held controllers. ³G_n_r_l_y speaking, they are easy to use, and you really feel like they are responding to your movements, especially in games where you explore space.

d _____

⁴By and l_ _g_, virtual reality headsets are incredibly heavy and cumbersome. It feels as if you are carrying a milk carton on your nose. Thankfully, the Oculus Rift is lightweight and comfortable.

e _____

In terms of sound quality, ⁵on the wh_ _ _, the headset is excellent. ⁶As a r_ _e, I like to use my own headphones with gadgets, and I was pleased that it was simple to hook these up to the device.

f _____

⁷Ov_r_ _l, the Oculus Rift is the ultimate gaming experience. The only danger is that you forget that there is another real world out there!

B Complete the paragraph headings (a–f) with 1–6.
1 Pleasant to wear
2 It feels as if you're really there
3 Remember there's a real world, too!
4 An exciting new device
5 Quickly reacts to hand actions
6 Compatible with other devices

C Complete the missing letters in the phrases for generalizing 1–7.

D Write your own conclusion to the product review in **A**. Do you think the Oculus Rift headset will catch on and become popular?

_____
_____

E Look back at lessons 4.1–4.5 in the Student's Book. Find the connection between the song lines and the content of each lesson.

F ◉17 Listen to the five question titles from the unit, and record your answers to them. If possible, compare recordings with a classmate.

5 » 5.1 What's your biggest life decision so far?

A ▶18 Match the sentence halves. There's one extra ending. Listen to the start of a podcast to check.

1 Golden Globe Award-winning actor Peter Dinklage has
2 However, like many actors, he had to overcome extreme
3 Moreover, as a "dwarf" (properly known as a "little person" today), Dinklage faced many
4 In fact, he had to say "no" to many early acting roles in order to pursue

a ☐ difficulties in finding decent parts to play.
b ☐ poverty at the beginning of his career.
c ☐ worked in a train station and as a waiter among other jobs.
d ☐ his dream of becoming a serious actor.
e ☐ achieved unbelievable success.

B ▶19 Listen to the whole podcast. Check (✓) the correct answers.

1 Dinklage's mom
  a ☐ had the same job as his dad.
  b ☐ worked in education.
  c ☐ was an actress.
2 Dinklage decided to become an actor
  a ☐ because he couldn't find any other work.
  b ☐ by chance.
  c ☐ when he was still a child.
3 In his early career, Dinklage refused to play
  a ☐ roles in commercial films.
  b ☐ fantasy characters.
  c ☐ comedy roles.
4 When he was a poor actor, his apartment
  a ☐ had animals living in it.
  b ☐ was incredibly hot.
  c ☐ was a long way away from the station.
5 According to the podcast, Dinklage's biggest decision was
  a ☐ accepting the role in *The Station Agent*.
  b ☐ leaving New Jersey.
  c ☐ refusing to play terrible roles.

C ▶19 Complete the sentences with a number. Listen again to check.

1 Dinklage was born in New Jersey in _____ .
2 He was in _____ grade when he heard his first big round of applause in a school play.
3 Dinklage says he often paid for his dinner in dimes – _____ cent pieces – because that was all he had.
4 In _____ , he starred in the movie *The Station Agent*.
5 His performance in *The Station Agent* was stunning, and won him a Golden Globe at the age of _____ .

D Cross out the incorrect option in each sentence.

1
It's not always easy in life to pursue your *ambition / goals / wish*.

2
We all face *destruction / obstacles / difficulties* in life. We have to confront them.

3
Work hard and you will achieve *a lot of money / good results / success*.

4
Learn to overcome your *fear of / luck at / problem with* the unknown.

23

» 5.2 What would you love to be able to do?

A ▶ 20 Complete the article with the correct form of the verbs. Listen to check.

Wishlist: What would you love to be able to do?

Kayleigh Bloom

That's easy – go surfing! If only my family ¹_____ (live) next to the ocean. People think everyone in Australia spends all day on the beach, but we live in Alice Springs, in the middle of the country. I couldn't live further from the coast.

How I wish my mom and dad ²_____ (have) a different job! My parents are farmers, and we have a farm with over 1,000 sheep, so we can't go anywhere else. Some days I wish they ³_____ (never / move) here. I wish I ⁴_____ (be) born in Sydney or somewhere like that.

If only I ⁵_____ (know) people with a house near the beach, then I could stay with them from time to time. I did have a friend who moved to Sydney and I wish I ⁶_____ (not / lost) contact with her. That would be perfect – Bondi Beach in the morning! Surf's up! If only …

B Correct the mistake in each sentence.

1 I wish I can swim. I can't believe I never learned. _____

2 My mom is always calling me on my cell phone. I wish she would do that! _____

3 I wish I didn't drop out of college. It was such a big mistake. _____

4 If only I have my credit card with me today, but I don't. _____

5 Rick always ignores me. If only he had replied to my emails from time to time. _____

6 I wish Martin hadn't put that terrible photo online, but he does, and now everyone has seen it. _____

C Circle the correct alternatives.

1 A: I'm never going to win the triathlon.
   B: Don't worry about winning. *Do / Make* the best you can.

2 A: This song is driving me crazy. I'm never going to learn how to play it.
   B: Keep *to / at* it! It takes time to learn these things.

3 A: I've applied for 50 jobs, and I haven't even had an interview.
   B: It's a bad time to look for work. Don't let it *get / getting* you down.

4 A: I think this course is a waste of time. I'm not learning anything new.
   B: Stick *in / with* it! You may be surprised what you learn by the end.

5 A: My presentation was a disaster. People were falling asleep listening to me!
   B: It happens to us all. *You / You'll* do better next time.

D Make it personal Write a true sentence about you to provoke these responses.

1 YOU: _____
   B: Do the best you can.

2 YOU: _____
   B: You'll do better next time.

How important is a college degree? 5.3 «

A Read and complete the article with these words. There are two extra words.

| international   overall   overestimate   overrated   overworked   underachievers |
| underestimate   underachievers   underpaid   underprivileged   underqualified |

"I don't want to go to school" "OK, then, don't!"

IT pioneers Bill Gates and Steve Jobs famously dropped out of college, but many never went to school at all. Instead, these kids were home-schooled, taught at home by their brave moms and dads, or by a specialist tutor.

There isn't much of an [1]_____ movement encouraging home-schooling worldwide because in many countries, it's simply illegal. However, it is common in the U.S., where there are around 1.8 million home-schooled children. Indeed, several experts warn we may [2]_____ those numbers because many states don't require parents to register their children at all. There may well be a lot more.

Parents usually choose home-schooling because they feel their children are [3]_____ , due to too much testing and homework in the current school system. Unfortunately, like it or not, tests equal results. Quite a few home-schooled children end their education [4]_____ because they have no full high school diploma.

But it cuts both ways. Some students, on the other hand, who were [5]_____ at school because of bullying, see a rapid improvement in their schoolwork when they start home-schooling. But what about the social side of things? Well, it's not necessarily a lonely life. People [6]_____ the difficulty of making friends, but there are lots of sports teams and clubs where home-schooled children can meet other kids.

Whatever the benefits, however, at the end of the day, home-schooling will never be an option for children from [7]_____ backgrounds. If their parents earn low salaries, and [8]_____, they simply cannot afford to take time off from work to educate their children themselves. So, yet again, the rich get richer.

B Complete 1–6 with a form of the word in CAPITALS.

1 I feel that teachers are _____underpaid_____ . They deserve a much higher salary. PAID

2 Don't _____ this physics problem. Your essay must show how complicated it is. SIMPLIFY

3 The city college is really _____. Their courses are actually very good. RATED

4 My grandma is one of life's _____. She left school at 15, but she now runs a chain of 12 stores. ACHIEVERS

5 I failed my audition for drama school. They said I was _____. I was shouting and screaming, and my character didn't feel natural. ACTING

6 Our end-of-course project was a disaster. We _____ how much time we needed, and we almost didn't finish it. ESTIMATED

C Correct the mistake in each sentence.

1 James has hardly no work experience. _____

2 Reading academic journals isn't exactly interested. _____

3 My granddad has virtually none qualifications. _____

4 Studying for an online degree is nothing but easy. _____

25

5.4 Did you make any mistakes yesterday?

A Read the article below. Check (✓) the correct column.

	What Mr. Sabo intended to do	What Mr. Sabo actually did
1 wear his glasses		
2 buy a ticket from a cashier		
3 buy a ticket from a machine		
4 get one $30 ticket		
5 get two $20 tickets		

B Re-read. T (true) or F (false)?

1 Mr. Sabo doesn't mind waiting for things.
2 He frequently uses the machines in the store.
3 He spent less money than he intended.
4 He immediately realized that he was a winner.
5 Other people share in Mr. Sabo's success.
6 The store has recently closed down.

Oops ... I think I'm a winner

All eyeglass wearers have done it; put down our glasses and then completely forgotten where they were. Like Bob Sabo, but, ironically, if he'd found his glasses last week, he'd be a lot poorer now. Why? Easton, Connecticut resident Mr. Sabo left home without them, and won $30,000 as a result.

Mr. Sabo wouldn't have his hands on the $30,000 check if he hadn't gotten impatient in his local Super Shop & Stop store. There was a long line at the cash register so, for the first time, he used a machine in the store to buy his lottery ticket.

Mr. Sabo had wanted to buy his usual two $20 tickets, but accidentally pressed the button for one $30 ticket. If he'd pressed the right button, our story would end there, but Mr. Sabo had found the Midas touch. When he got home, he discovered that he was holding a winning ticket for $30,000! If he'd had his glasses on, his wallet would be a lot lighter today.

As a reward for selling the ticket, the store also gets $300 and all the publicity in the world. So, glasses or no glasses, it looks like those lines at the cash register aren't going to go away anytime soon.

C Complete the sentences with the correct form of the verbs.

1 If I _____ (not be) a native speaker of Portuguese, I wouldn't have gotten my job.
2 Just think! If you _____ (chose) 17 instead of 16, you would have won the lottery. You were so close to $500,000!
3 We _____ (live) in Japan today if our parents hadn't emigrated to Brazil back in 1999.
4 An old friend got in contact after 10 years. He _____ (not find) me online if I weren't on Facebook.
5 Aziz _____ (drive) you to the station tomorrow if he hadn't had that car accident last week.
6 My brother was so close to dropping out of college in 2011. Think about that. He _____ (not work) as a doctor now if he had.

D Make it personal Have you ever sent or received an email, photo, text, or Whatsapp® message by mistake? What happened? How did you feel?

_____
_____

How lucky are you? 5.5

Telling a story (2)

A Read the story and order the pictures 1–5.

*Lightning doesn't strike the same place twice …
it can strike it seven times!*

Everything was tranquil out on the lake on that day in June, 1977. Park ranger Roy Sullivan was quietly fishing when he noticed an odd smell in the air, like sulfur. It was a warning.

Suddenly, a lightning bolt struck him with devastating force, and he fell out of his boat. Shocked and exhausted, Roy swam to the shore, but his ordeal was not yet over. Badly burned and with black holes in his clothes, he crawled back to his car. If he thought he was safe, he was in for another surprise.

To Roy's horror, he discovered a huge black bear right next to his vehicle. The bear had come out of the woods and was eating the fish that Roy had caught. Most people would have been terrified, but the ranger just took a tree branch and hit the bear in the face, which frightened the animal away. Finally, Roy was able to drive to hospital, after the luckiest – or unluckiest – day of his life.

What's most amazing about this story is that it wasn't the first time that Roy Sullivan had been hit by lightning. In fact, it was the seventh lighting strike that the park ranger had survived, earning him a place in the *Guinness Book of Records*. He also claimed to have encountered bears over 20 times during his legendary career at Shenandoah National Park. They don't make park rangers like they used to.

B Find vivid adjectives in the text which are synonyms for 1–8.

1 peaceful and quiet (para 1) _____
2 powerful and destructive (para 2) _____
3 surprised and scared (para 2) _____
4 really tired (paragraph 2) _____
5 extremely large (para 3) _____
6 extremely scared (para 3) _____
7 surprising, incredible (para 4) _____
8 very, very famous (para 4) _____

C Complete a short entry about Roy for an online wiki. Use at least two bold vivid adjectives from B.

Legendary park ranger Roy Sullivan (1912–1983) _____
_____
_____

D Look back at lessons 5.1–5.5 in the Student's Book. Find the connection between the song lines and the content of each lesson.

E ▶21 Listen to the five question titles from this unit, and record your answers to them. If possible, compare recordings with a classmate.

6 » 6.1 Have you ever Googled yourself?

A Cross out the option that doesn't work in each sentence.
1 We're worried about *journalists / hackers / teachers* entering the school website.
2 Someone broke into my *bag / car / website*, but I don't know if it's worth telling the police.
3 She was surprised when she looked *herself / the definition / the password* up online.
4 *Doctors / Flight attendants / Teachers* always keep records of the people they work with.

B ▶22 Listen to Isabella's tech tips and number these search engines in the order you hear them 1–4. What's the main topic of her broadcast?
1 what's wrong with Google® ☐
2 how Google became the world's top search engine ☐
3 Google's competitors ☐

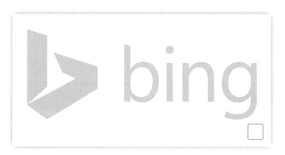

C ▶22 Complete 1–4 with the search engines in **B**. Listen again to check, if necessary.
1 _____ is currently the most popular search engine.
2 _____ helps you maintain privacy when searching online.
3 _____ is pretty similar to Google.
4 _____ helps people find text and pictures that they don't have to pay for.

D ▶22 Listen again. Check (✓) the two conclusions you can draw from Isabella.
1 Most search engines have both advantages and disadvantages. ☐
2 People should stop using Google immediately. ☐
3 It's far too risky to use more than one search engine on their computer. ☐
4 Google is fine, but you might want to use others from time to time. ☐

E Add *is* four times to this quote.

> "The biggest risk not taking any risk … In a world that changing really quickly, the only strategy that guaranteed to fail not taking risks."
>
> Mark Zuckerberg (Founder of Facebook)

Do you worry about your privacy? 6.2 «

A Rewrite what these people said using the passive form. Include the word in CAPITALS.

1 Someone took a video from my YouTube® account and used it without my permission. TAKEN

_____

2 Somebody hacked my blog, so when people looked at it, they saw an ad for second-hand cell phones. HAD

_____

3 It would shock you if you Googled yourself. BE

_____

4 My friends have put lots of photos of me on Facebook. BY

_____

5 A group of people are spreading a rumor about you on Twitter. BEING

_____

6 Nick asked a programmer to design his website for him. WAS

_____

B ▶ 23 Complete the conversation with these phrases. There's one extra. Listen to check.

| point taken   I don't see it that way   here's the thing   I admit |
| what's your take on it   couldn't agree more   believe it or not |

ADAM: Listen to this. A 22-year-old woman, Connor Riley, was offered a job by a major IT company. Immediately afterwards, she went on Twitter and complained she didn't like the trip to the office and hated the work. The company saw the tweet, and ¹_____ fired her before she started work!

KIRSTY: Whoa, Adam! That's not fair!

ADAM: Are you kidding? ²_____ . She insulted her new company. What kind of employee is that?

KIRSTY: ³_____ . Twitter is private! Why should her company be looking at her tweets?

ADAM: Twitter isn't private! That's why employees of big companies have to write things like "All opinions are my own" when they use it.

KIRSTY: OK, ⁴_____ , but I still think it's an invasion of privacy. Jason, ⁵_____ ?

JASON: Me? Well, I feel sorry for her. She makes one mistake at 22, and it's on the Internet forever.

ADAM: Absolutely! I ⁶_____ . That's why you have to be so careful about what you put online.

C Correct one mistake in each conversation.

1 A: I don't think people should use their smartphones when they're talking to you.
  B: I'm totally agree. It's really rude, isn't it? _____

2 A: I think we should ask for some help in designing our website. I don't think we can do it on our own.
  B: That does sense, I admit. _____

3 A: Listen to what I'm about saying. It's very important.
  B: OK. I'm all ears! _____

4 A: Why don't you want to be on Facebook?
  B: Look, here the thing. I don't want to tell everybody about everything I'm doing. I value my privacy.

  _____

5 A: If you try to write your essay in the middle of the night, you're going to make mistakes. Take your time with it.
  B: OK, OK! Point take. _____

D **Make it personal** Describe a time when someone you know wrote an inappropriate online post. What happened?

_____

_____

6.3 What makes you suspicious?

A Read the newspaper article. Check (✓) the correct question 1–3.

Digital Detective

Do you have a problem and no one else can help? Email it to … the Digital Detective!

1 Am I right to keep tabs on my son?
2 Are we being spied on through the computer?
3 Is the government eavesdropping on our online conversations?

Dear Digital Detective

My husband and I bought our 12-year old son his first computer, and he loves it. He's designing his own games, and he's set up a blog. We're so happy that he's enjoying writing ¹**it**, but there's just one problem. The computer's a laptop with a built-in camera, and our son's convinced he's being watched through it. He won't believe me when I say it's OK. Can you help me set his mind at rest?

Concerned mom

The Digital Detective replies …

It's natural to be afraid of being connected to almost everyone on the planet via the Internet. Personally, I'd be pleased that your son is conscious of these dangers. Many people his age are unaware of ²**them**.

Having said that, the camera is a threat. It's possible for other people to take control of this device. ³**They** break into your computer in the traditional way: using a virus on a website, so you need to ensure your antivirus is up-to-date. Also check that you have a password for your home WiFi, and make sure it's ⁴**one** that's hard to crack, because that's also a vulnerability.

You'll know if your webcam is active because a blue light appears when you're using it (look for ⁵**this** next time you make a call). If you don't see a light, it's unlikely anyone else is there.

If you're still concerned, there's one very basic way of avoiding unwanted surveillance. When you're not using the webcam, cover it up with a sock or a piece of paper. ⁶**That** will give them a black screen to stare at!

B What do the bold words in the article refer to?
1 ___his blog___
2 _____
3 _____
4 _____
5 _____
6 _____

C Check (✓) the sentences that you can infer from the article.

The Digital Detective …
1 has some sympathy for the son. ☐
2 doesn't think teenagers appreciate the risks presented by the Internet. ☐
3 believes that there is a solution to every online threat. ☐
4 thinks that almost every home computer is infected with a virus. ☐
5 enjoys low-tech solutions to high-tech problems. ☐

D Read the graffiti, then complete the sentence so that it expresses your opinion.

Suspicion is the cancer of friendship.
Suspicion and doubt lead to animosity and hatred.
Secrets don't destroy things, but suspicion does.
Suspicion often creates what it suspects.

For me, suspicion _____.

Are you into social media? 6.4

A Read the article below and check (✓) the best summary.

1 A supermarket worker posted a question on the Internet and made thousands of new friends. ☐
2 An ordinary guy became famous because a customer where he worked thought he was attractive and tweeted his photo. ☐

B ▶24 Re-read and circle the correct alternatives. Listen to check.

Alex from Target becomes the Target!

"There's one thing in life worse than being talked about, and that's not being talked about."
[1]*Whenever / Whichever* the Irish author Oscar Wilde said that, it clearly wasn't during the Internet age. It's one thing for a celebrity to face media exposure, but [2]*whichever / whoever* thought that the full glare of public interest could fall on an everyday supermarket employee?

Alex Lee was working at his local Target supermarket when a teenage girl, struck by his good looks, snapped his photo. [3]*However / Whatever* it happened, the image turned up on Tumblr®, and then Twitter with the hashtag #Alexfromtarget. It created a Twitter frenzy with 800,000 retweets over the course of the day. [4]*Whichever / Whoever* site you looked at, Alex was trending.

[5]*However / Whatever* else Alex was doing that day, he wasn't expecting to become world famous. It was only at the end of his shift that he checked his cell phone and discovered he had thousands of new followers. His innocent next tweet then went viral:

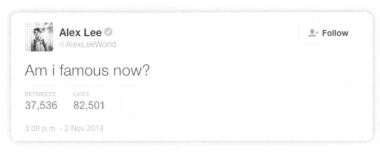

the bemused worker wondered.

The answer is yes – and he's now seeking a career as a musician with his own site on YouTube.

C Match 1–5 to a–f to make sentences. There is one extra ending.

1 I get my smartphone out and check Facebook
2 I never agree to be online friends with someone I haven't met
3 I'm pretty patient. I'll wait to connect to the WiFi
4 Photo quality is never great online
5 I never reply to Twitter abuse

a ☐ whichever site you use to upload them.
b ☐ whenever I'm on public transportation.
c ☐ whatever they say about me.
d ☐ however long it takes.
e ☐ whatever you like.
f ☐ whoever they are.

D **Make it personal** Complete the sentences so they're true for you.

1 I go online whenever _____.
2 I use my smartphone to watch whatever _____.
3 Wherever I go, I keep my cell phone on, except _____.

6.5 Who do you share your secrets with?

A how to ... guide

How to keep your smartphone safe

Almost everyone has an anti-virus program on their computer, but large numbers of people have no security protection on their smartphone. So how can you keep your smartphone safe? Here are six top tips.

A _____

As
[1]~~So~~ far as possible, use the latest updates for your phone. Even if you don't have an anti-virus, this will ensure that the major security holes stay closed.

B _____

[2]Never not ever click on a link in a text message or email from an unknown source. This is one of the most common ways of inserting malware – dangerous programs – onto your handheld device.

C _____

Get a "find my phone" app. This will tell you where your phone is if it gets lost. [3]However you do, do not approach someone who has stolen your phone. This can be a dangerous situation.

D _____

Lock your screen with a password. [4]Avoid to use programs that don't have a password with letters, numbers, and symbols.

E _____

If you use your phone for online shopping, [5]be sure use a site with a "https" in the address bar, like https://www.amazon.com. The final -s indicates that it is secure.

F _____

[6]Make your best to use private, not public, WiFi networks. Unwanted listeners may be eavesdropping on your conversations.

A Read the article and check (✓) what you think is the most important tip (A–F).

B Re-read and correct the mistakes in the underlined phrases 1–6.

C Match the headings 1–7 to paragraphs A–F. There's one extra.

1 Make it difficult to log on to your device.
2 Never use your real name.
3 Don't respond to strangers when they contact you.
4 Avoid going online in cafés and public places.
5 Keep your smartphone up-to-date.
6 Look carefully at the URL before you buy.
7 Find your phone with an app.

D Add one more guideline to explain how to keep your smartphone safe.

_____

_____

_____

E Look back at lessons 6.1–6.5 in the Student's Book. Find the connection between the song lines and the content of each lesson.

F ▶ 25 Listen to the five question titles from the unit, and record your answers to them. If possible, compare recordings with a classmate.

32

7 » 7.1   How important is music to you?

A Complete the biography with these words. There are two extra words.

came	high-profile	large	lost	regarded	released	rose	took

Taylor Swift is ¹_____ as one of the finest singer-songwriters of the decade. Born in Reading, Pennsylvania on December 13th, 1989, she moved to Nashville, Tennessee at the age of 14 to pursue a career in country music. She ²_____ to fame through the hit *Our Song*, which she wrote when she was still a teenager. She became the youngest songwriter ever signed by Sony® and ³_____ her debut album, *Taylor Swift*, when she was only 16. By the time her second album *Fearless* ⁴_____ out in 2007, she was already one of the biggest stars on the U.S. rock and pop scene. It was named album of the year at the Grammys, making her the youngest-ever winner of the award.

As a ⁵_____ figure in the music industry, Swift is also prepared to speak out on important issues, such as the payment of royalties by Apple® for online downloads. This dispute ⁶_____ place in 2015 when a single online letter from Swift changed Apple's policy in just one day. As someone who was fighting for the rights of less successful artists, Swift gained even more fans for her brave act in standing up to big business. Her fifth album, *1989*, was the world's second-biggest seller in 2015, beaten only by Adele's *25*.

B 🔘26 Circle the correct alternatives. Listen to check.

LISA: I've ¹*done / had* enough of this album. You play it all the time.

SHANE: I know, I'm sorry. For some reason, I just can't ²*get / make* enough of it.

LISA: What is it about you and Taylor Swift?

SHANE: Her music is amazing. I also like her because she's been on a similar musical path to me.

LISA: Yeah, right. You're hardly a multi-million-download-selling hit machine!

SHANE: I'm talking about musical styles. Taylor Swift started her career as a country and western singer. Then she changed to pop. Well, when I was a kid, I was really fond ³*about / of* country music. My mom and dad were in a band, and we listened to country all the time. They were the New Jersey Cowboys.

LISA: You're kidding!

SHANE: Not at all! They were really good. Anyway, eventually I ⁴*got / took* tired of listening to all those songs, and I started listening to other things. Now, I'm hooked ⁵*in / on* rock, and I think Taylor Swift is one of the best performers out there.

LISA: I don't know. I'm more ⁶*into / onto* funky stuff like Bruno Mars. In fact, I'm switching tracks now. It's time for a bit of *Uptown Funk*!

SHANE: Fine, but I'll change it back as soon as you go out!

C **Make it personal** Complete these sentences about musical tastes so they're true for you.

When I was a kid, I was fond _____ , but now I'm hooked _____ .

I never get tired of _____ . I can't get enough _____ .

33

7.2 What was your most recent disappointment?

A Match 1–6 to a–h to make a story. There are two extra endings.

1 We were determined to see Adele in concert since
2 The concert was on the same day as my eldest daughter's birthday, so
3 On the day, we were late for the concert because of
4 Then my youngest daughter couldn't see much because
5 I put her on my shoulders so that
6 We loved it, but we can't go to her next concert due to

a ☐ all the cars on the road.
b ☐ the high price of the tickets.
c ☐ I decided to get some tickets as a present.
d ☐ there were so many tall people in front of her.
e ☐ the tickets were too expensive.
f ☐ she was able to see the stage.
g ☐ there were so many cars on the road.
h ☐ she hadn't toured in years.

B Read and cross out the incorrect choice for 1–6.

What was your most recent disappointment?

Last month and it was massive! All my life I had wanted to see the musical *Cats*, but it had been impossible ¹*as / since / so that* the producers had stopped the shows back in the year 2000. ²*Because / Because of / As* I heard they were bringing it back to the stage this year, I was determined to see it.

We bought the tickets, and we were all ready to go to Broadway to see it on Thanksgiving. That morning, my dad was putting some pictures up ³*due to / in order to / to* make the house look nice before our grandma visited the next day. Unfortunately, he put a nail right through a water pipe. Water was pouring into the living room. It was a disaster, and we couldn't find a plumber ⁴*because of / due to / since* the holiday. We waited for ages and ended up missing the show. My dad promised to get new tickets ⁵*in order to / so / so that* we could go another day, but *Cats* was only on for a limited time. ⁶*As / Because of / Due to* that, I never got to see the show. What a bitter disappointment!

C Correct the mistake in each sentence. One sentence is correct.

1 I didn't buy a ticket for the concert, so I didn't hear about it in time. _____
2 We set off early in order beat the morning rush-hour traffic. _____
3 They postponed the final game due to the weather. _____
4 I'm going to the supermarket for get some fruit. _____
5 So that he was so unfit, his doctor advised him to go to the gym twice a week. _____

What's the best movie you've ever seen? 7.3 «

A Read the article. T (true) or F (false)?

1 Movies that critics really don't like are certain to be unpopular with the general public.

2 Some movies might fail in the U.S. but, nevertheless, be very successful in the rest of the world.

B Re-read and complete 1–5 with the missing sentences a–e.

a 2013's *After Earth* is another classic example.

b Anything that originally came from a comic seems like box-office gold.

c Not such a bad piece of business after all.

d they are unbelievably expensive to make

e While they often disagree,

Think they're flops? Actually they're not!

[1]_____ , there are some movies that the critics unanimously hate. As soon as they hit the big screen, the attack begins. It doesn't take long for a movie to get a reputation as a complete **dud** – but actually many movies that people think are flops have made a huge amount of money.

One of the most famous disasters of all time was 1995's *Waterworld*. This movie takes place in the future after the Antarctic has **melted** and the world is almost completely underwater. It was hugely expensive to make, and people said it lost a fortune. However, a flop it was not – *Waterworld* eventually made a **profit** of $91 million. [2]_____

Nowadays, superhero movies are a license to print money. [3]_____ Back in 2006, they weren't such a **guaranteed** hit. That year's *Superman Returns* was widely considered to be a failure, but it too made around $130 million. If that's a failure, give some to me!

The key thing here is that these are worldwide hits. Some of these movies failed at home in the U.S., but drew enormous audiences **overseas**. [4]_____ This adventure on a distant planet starred real-life father and son Will and Jaden Smith. While U.S. audiences stayed at home, the movie made $182 million in the rest of the world. Strangely, even Will Smith considers the film to be a disaster, despite its global success.

It's no coincidence that these are all science-fiction movies. Because of their special effects, [5]_____ . If they don't make instant millions, it's easy to say that they are failures, especially during their opening weekend. Nevertheless, it's increasingly obvious that the media isn't always right: when they label a movie a flop, a lot of times, it's not.

C Match the bold words in the article to definitions 1–5.

1 money you earn from something _____

2 a movie that is a flop, not a success _____

3 definite, certain _____

4 changed from a solid to a liquid _____

5 in other countries _____

D ▶27 Complete 1–5 with these words. There's one extra. Listen to check.

| backfired | caught on | didn't live up to | failed to | lacked | surprised |

1 The restaurant hoped that people would love their super-spicy pizza with extra chili, but it never _____ . Nobody seemed to like it.

2 The musical was OK, but it _____ really powerful songs. What it really needed were some catchy ones for audiences to sing along with.

3 We thought that the concert was going to be amazing, but sadly it _____ our expectations. Really disappointing.

4 Stacey posted a photo on Facebook of me singing to make fun of me – but her plan _____ . Everybody loved it. I got over 100 likes!

5 The band's first album _____ impress people, but their second album was a huge hit!

35

7.4 When was the last time you went to a museum?

A ▶ 28 Listen to a podcast between James and Adriana about an exhibit at the Tate Modern art gallery in London. Number the verbs in the order you hear them (1–4).

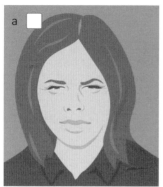
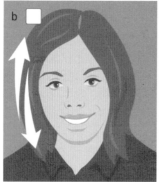
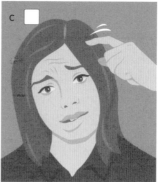

B ▶ 28 Listen again. T (true) or F (false)?
1 Adriana is a fan of Modern Art.
2 The Tate Modern building has always been an art gallery.
3 The slide was invented by a British artist.
4 In the beginning, the kids didn't have enough tickets for the slide.
5 You have to wear protective clothing on the slide.
6 James wanted to go on the slide several times.
7 The slide is art because it makes people feel strong emotions.
8 The slide has only appeared in museums in Europe.

C Correct the mistake in each sentence. One sentence is correct.
1 We have another students in our class today. _____
2 Some other people was in the gallery at the same time as us. _____
3 Do you like this painting or the others ones? _____
4 I can't meet at 4 p.m. Can you meet at other time? _____
5 I like the hotels in the city center, but I don't like the other. They're too far away. _____
6 My son made friends with some other children when we were on holiday. _____
7 Can you help me, please? There's another problem with the computer. _____
8 Harry is going to study medicine – and I have some others news for you, too. _____

36

Which musician do you listen to most? 7.5 «

Writing a review

A Complete the review with the adverb form of these words.

| absolute | clever | consistent | disappoint | easy | firm | huge | ~~incredible~~ | occasion | surprise |

George Ezra – Live in Spain!

A George Ezra's biggest hit *Budapest* has already gotten 113 million listens on Spotify®, and 1 _incredibly_ he's still only 23.

B Barcelona 2_____ gets big acts playing in the city, such as Coldplay and U2. They play in enormous venues like the Nou Camp, FC Barcelona's stadium. However, Ezra was in the Sala Bikini, a 3_____ small place for someone with his online success. We were just five meters from the stage in a room that was as big as a restaurant. It was 4_____ the closest I've ever been to such a big star in concert.

C We arrived late, so 5_____ we missed the support act, but Ezra came on stage right on time. The opening song was *Cassy O*, the fastest track from his 6_____ successful album *Wanted on Voyage*. The crowd was rocking from the start.

D His voice was 7_____ amazing throughout the whole concert. We loved the gig. The two highlights of the night were *Budapest*, of course, as well as *Barcelona*. Ezra wrote the song about a visit to our city, and 8_____ he left it till the very end.

E Live, Ezra is 9_____ incredible, and I 10_____ believe that in the future he's going to be a mega-star. Get to see him in small venues while you still can!

B In which paragraph A–E do you find the answers to 1–6? One question is not answered.

1 What albums has George Ezra recorded? ☐
2 What were the best parts of the concert? ☐
3 What nationality is George Ezra? ☐
4 Where can you see live music in Barcelona? ☐

5 Does the author recommend seeing George Ezra in concert? ☐
6 How old was George Ezra when he played in Barcelona? ☐

C **Make it personal** Write a one-paragraph review of a concert you saw. Include this information: Who? Where? When? Best parts?

_____

_____

_____

D Look back at lessons 7.1–7.5 in the Student's Book. Find the connection between the song lines and the content of each lesson.

E ◉29 Listen to the five question titles from the unit, and record your answers to them. If possible, compare recordings with a classmate.

37

8 » 8.1   Has fear ever held you back?

A Combine ideas 1–6 into single sentences using the words in CAPITALS.

1 I have a fear of flying. I cannot get on a plane. TERRIFIED
   I'm terrified of flying.

2 I think prawns are disgusting. They look like insects to me. FREAK / OUT

3 I don't have a problem with snakes. Unlike many people. BOTHER / ME

4 You can bring your dog when you stay with us. I really like them. MIND / AT ALL

5 I try not to give presentations on my job. I get too nervous. AVOID

6 I always feel uncomfortable around spiders. I don't know why. MAKE / BIT / UNEASY

B ▶30 Complete the blog with these words. There are two extra. Listen to check.

| breathe   dizzy   fell   heart   neck   passed   stomach   sweat   tears |

Jabs needle me!

What a day! I'm off to South America next month and had to get a yellow fever vaccination. I'd been panicking about it for weeks as I have a total phobia of needles. My ¹_____ starts to race just thinking about injections because of a really nasty experience at school.

When I was about 14, we all had to have a BCG injection against tuberculosis, and the nurse was horrible. She made us watch each person in turn get the injection. I waited, terrified, staring at injection after injection. I almost ²_____ out in terror. In the end, I burst into ³_____ , and all the other kids laughed at me.

So today was awful. My girlfriend, Susie, came with me, but I started to ⁴_____ even before we got to the doctor's. My shirt was wet as if it was 35°C outside. While we were waiting, I got terrible butterflies in my ⁵_____ . I wanted to run out the door, but Susie forced me to stay.

Finally, the doctor called me in. When I saw the needle, I got really ⁶_____ . My head was spinning. I couldn't ⁷_____ – I wanted my asthma inhaler, but then something amazing happened. As the doctor was chatting with me, she walked behind me. Before I knew it, the injection was over, in a flash! So, Amazon rainforest – here we come!

C **Make it personal** Complete the sentences so they're true for you.

1 When I see a needle, I _____ .

2 Once I burst into tears because _____ .

3 I often get butterflies in my stomach before _____ .

38

Are you good at improvising? 8.2

A ▶31 Listen to a conversation about Niihau, Hawaii's "forbidden island." Who said 1–6: M (Martina) or L (Luca)?

1 For many years, tourists couldn't go to Niihau at all. ☐
2 Are you telling me you were able to visit this place? ☐
3 Were you able to meet any of the locals? ☐
4 Our limit was three hours. ☐
5 I was just able to take a photo before it disappeared under the water. ☐
6 I don't think I could have done it on my own. ☐

B ▶31 Correct one word in each sentence. Listen again to check.

1 That's because it's one of the most unpleasant places in the world to visit. _____
2 In the past, you could only go there if you worked there. _____
3 I managed to go there by boat with my parents. _____
4 No one speaks English on the island. _____
5 The sea is crystal clear, and the beaches have wonderful golden sand. _____
6 There are only a few trips to Niihau every month. _____
7 My company paid for me to go there. It was very expensive. _____
8 It was the most terrifying experience of my life. _____

C Complete conversations 1–5 with *could* or *was able to*. Use both when possible.

1 A: Did you see that Nicky was on TV last night?
   B: Yeah! I _____ believe it!
2 A: Are you having a nice stay in L.A.?
   B: Yes, the hotel has a cool pool, so I _____ have a great swim yesterday.
3 A: Mom, what was my first word?
   B: Well, you _____ speak at about 18 months old, and as far as I remember, it was "daddy."
4 A: Did you get Jimi's birthday present?
   B: Yes, just! I got to the store as it was closing, so I _____ quickly buy him a book.
5 A: Where have you been? Did you get lost?
   B: Yeah, we _____ get the sat-nav to work in the car. I think it's broken.

D Make it personal Write true answers to these questions.

1 Was there anything you could do as a child that you can't do now?
   _____

2 Was there anything you weren't able to do last year that you really wanted to do?
   _____

>> 8.3   How much attention do you pay to the news?

A Circle the correct alternatives.

1 News editors, photojournalists, and TV producers have to *carry out / cope with* the stress of seeing disturbing images as part of their jobs.

2 Nevertheless, when something bad is happening, the media has a responsibility to *spread / carry out* the news.

3 More and more violence is appearing on TV, and studies need to be *boosted / carried out* to learn how these changes are affecting our society.

4 The use of extreme scenes is a cynical way of *boosting / coping with* a show's ratings.

5 That is how rumors are *boosted / spread*.

6 Many viewers of the news may be *spreading / undergoing* treatment with medical professionals for stress-related illnesses.

B Read and complete the webpage, with topic sentences 1–6 from **A**. There's one extra.

How real should the news be?

A_____ It's especially a problem in drama where almost every series contains graphic images with little warning for the viewer. Whatever the conclusions of future research, it seems clear that things that were shocking for our grandparents have become an everyday occurrence in modern drama.

B_____ It gets everybody talking about the series, both with their friends and on social media. Newspapers run stories about it pretending to criticize the action while printing photos of the most explicit scenes. The public seems to have an insatiable appetite for this kind of violence. But what about real violence and real suffering?

C_____ Indeed, they come across much worse scenes every day than they ultimately show to the public. They then edit these for broadcast. Now the question is, how graphic should the news be? Should they show the true horror of violence that professionals in the field encounter? Clearly, the answer has to be "no".

D_____ Unlike in a drama where people know what kind of images they are likely to see, any viewer can just switch on the news. Seeing graphic images of violence without warning can badly affect people who have lived through terrible events in their own lives. Shocking images can bring back their own experiences.

E_____ Otherwise, the public can close its eyes and pretend that the troubles of the world aren't really happening. This leads to a difficult balancing act for TV producers and newspaper editors. On the one hand, they are presenting news for an "unshockable" public that is used to seeing graphic images. On the other, they have a responsibility towards younger and more impressionable viewers. This tension is what prevents the news from being as "real" as it could be.

C Use the clues to complete the puzzle. What is the adjective in gray?

1 Failed TV stars will go on any old reality show to boost their _____ with the public.

2 Singing in front of an audience for the first time has boosted my _____ enormously. I now really believe in myself.

3 I told my granddad that I would get into medical school, and I'm determined to carry out the _____ that I made to him.

4 Our company is undergoing a lot of _____ at the moment. Things are different from one day to the next.

5 Janine has been spreading _____ about me. She told everyone that I'd been stealing from the company, and it's just not true.

6 I'm finding it difficult to cope with the _____ of bringing up two small children. Being a mother is the hardest job in the world.

40

What prevents you from traveling more? 8.4 «

A Match 1–4 to a–e to complete the sentences. There's one extra ending.

1 You aren't allowed to drive when you're taking this medication. It's a
2 You can use cell phones, but you can't use laptops on planes. That just seems contradictory. It's a
3 Technically, it's forbidden to use your cell phone at customs, but they don't
4 In most countries, you have to carry an ID card at all times. It's

a ☐ enforce the law.   c ☐ pointless law.   e ☐ required by law.
b ☐ got to obey.   d ☐ violation of the law.

B Check (✓) the signs that match the rules. Correct those that don't.

| 1 | 2 | 3 | 4 | 5 | 6 |

1 You're supposed to eat here. ☐ _____
2 No dogs are allowed on the beach. ☐ _____
3 You'd better watch out for penguins while you're driving. ☐ _____
4 You don't have to swim here. ☐ _____
5 You should drink the tap water. ☐ _____
6 Only disabled people aren't allowed to park here. ☐ _____

C ▶32 Complete the conversations with these words. There's one extra. Listen to check.

| 're allowed to   aren't supposed to   must not   'd better   don't have to   ought to |

1 A: I ate that last sandwich in the fridge, and now I've found out that it was Ella's!
   B: Well, you _____ not tell her it was you. She'll be furious.
2 A: Do I need to wear a tie for the meeting?
   B: No, you _____ . Everyone just wears casual clothes, but it's up to you.
3 A: I need to find my hotel reservation. Can I look up the address on your computer?
   B: Well, we _____ do that at work, but I guess it's OK, just this once. But don't tell anyone or I'll get in trouble!
4 A: Do you have any recommendations for things to do while I'm in Athens?
   B: You _____ go to the archaeological museum. It's amazing! And it's only about seven euros to get in!
5 A: Is it OK to use my cell phone here in the hospital?
   B: You _____ use them outside, in the corridors and café, but not on the wards themselves. Besides, it's often hard to get a signal.

D **Make it personal** Complete 1–5 to make true statements about your workplace / place of study.

1 We are / aren't supposed to _____ , but nobody does it.
2 Everyone is allowed to _____ .
3 We have to _____ every day.
4 At lunchtime, we can _____ .
5 You shouldn't _____ at any time.

41

≫ 8.5 Who do you usually turn to for advice?

A message of advice

A Read Ivana's response to George. Check (✓) the things that George mentioned in his previous message to Ingrid.

George ...

1 asked her to give him some advice. ☐
2 told Ingrid he was feeling stressed. ☐
3 has a new job. ☐
4 has lots of friends where he lives. ☐

5 feels unwell because of his anxiety. ☐
6 loves doing all kinds of sports. ☐
7 feels tired all the time. ☐
8 doesn't use Skype®. ☐

So, if you have any advice, Ingrid, I'd love to hear it. Hope to hear from you soon.

George

Hi George

Lots of us suffer from anxiety. I [1]m__ __n it's normal to feel like this when you start out on a new career, like you are. Fortunately, there are lots of ways to combat this problem.

[2]F__ __ st__ __t__ __s, you're doing the right thing to ask for advice. Many people feel alone because they bottle these feelings up, [3]s__ t__ sp__ __k. Just talking about your fears can help you cope with them. It's a shame you have nobody close to you in your new home.

A common experience is physical symptoms of anxiety such as sweating and feeling dizzy. [4]Th__ __ sa__ __, many of us have difficulty breathing when we feel stressed, and you need to learn to control that. Breathing exercises can really help to calm you down. [5]T__ __ __t me, these will help to control those feelings of panic.

Another technique is to do some exercise. You said you enjoy running, so maybe you should go for a run now and then. When you live in the moment, you forget your worries for a while. [6]O__ __ __r th__ __ th__ __, when I feel anxious, I always take the dog for a walk, and that really helps.

In fact, living a healthy lifestyle is very important in terms of our mental health. Make simple changes. You said you weren't sleeping well even though you were often exhausted. You shouldn't drink coffee or tea or too many sodas. They contain caffeine, and they can stop you sleeping at night. [7]N__ __dl__ __ __ __ to s__ __, when you're anxious, you have to get plenty of rest.

If you want to talk about anything else, you can call me anytime, OK? [8]Th__ __ __ __ g__ __d__ __ __ __s we have Skype!

Ingrid

B Complete the missing letters in the phrases for making friendly comments.

C Underline the five pieces of advice Ingrid gives George. Then think of your own advice for George.

A couple of other things you could try doing are _____

and _____ .

D Look back at lessons 8.1–8.5 in the Student's Book. Find the connection between the song lines and the content of each lesson.

E ▶33 Listen to the five question titles from the unit, and record your answers to them. If possible, compare recordings with a classmate.

9 » 9.1 How much time do you spend on your own?

A Read and complete the article with these words and phrases. There are two extra words/phrases.

> keep quiet   mingle   open up   reveal   small talk   thinking it over   thinking out loud

How to survive at a wedding when you don't have anyone to go with

- First of all, you should [1]_____ when you arrive and chat with everyone you can. You'll be surprised how many other people also feel like strangers at an event like this.

- It's a mistake to [2]_____ when you're on your own. You have to initiate conversations and start talking.

- If you find it difficult to make [3]_____ , just ask lots of questions: *What do you do? How did you decide what to wear?*

- If you're embarrassed about being alone, just don't tell anyone. You don't have to [4]_____ any information about yourself. Anyway, what's wrong with being alone? Everyone's single at some point in his or her life.

- The hardest part is the dancing. My advice is to prepare for this early on. At the buffet or during the welcome drinks, do some [5]_____ about what you're going to do when all the couples are on the dance floor. Someone will hear you and is sure to be in the same situation. You'll soon find a non-dancing buddy to chat with while everyone else is having his or her romantic moment.

B ▶ 34 Order the words in B's responses to questions about plans for a wedding. Listen to check.

1 A: What do you think of Vicky's suggestion of San Francisco for your honeymoon?
   B: the / over / it / of / thinking / we're / process / in
   _____

2 A: How does Mike know about the bachelor party? It's supposed to be a secret.
   B: mistake / showed / invitation / him / by / I / the / to
   _____

3 A: Did you remember to get a gift for the wedding?
   B: last / we / present / a / week / them / sent / yeah
   _____

4 A: Where did you get this idea for the wedding invitations from?
   B: it / mom / thought / up / my
   _____

5 A: Did you remember to get in touch with everybody about his or her dietary requirements for the wedding?
   B: an / I'll / them / email / send / right away
   _____

6 A: How was the food tasting for the wedding?
   B: food / the / prepared / beautifully / caterers / the / absolutely
   _____

C **Make it personal** Complete the sentences so they're true for you.

1 When I need to think things over, I usually _____ .
2 When I have to make small talk, I usually _____ .
3 The best place/time to think up new ideas is _____ .

43

9.2 What behavior is rude in your culture?

A Look at the photo and think of two things you should and shouldn't do when in Dubai. Read the text to check your ideas.

B ▶35 Complete the tips with non-restrictive clauses (1–6). Listen to check.
1 which is why the malls are a top destination for visitors.
2 which makes it uncomfortable to be out at any time of day.
3 which means you'll probably visit it at some point if you're a business traveler.
4 which is a perfect time to meet local people as well as try the local cuisine.
5 which is one place where beach wear is acceptable.
6 which will make you feel like you're in a science-fiction movie!

Dos and Don'ts – Dubai, United Arab Emirates

Dubai, a city in the desert, is rapidly becoming a major transportation hub, A_____ . Whether there on a stopover, a vacation, or for business, here are five tips to make the most of the city.

Do
- Visit the Burj Khalifa. It's the world's tallest building made of glass and steel, B_____ .
- Go shopping. Shopping is a national pastime in Dubai, C_____ . They are like cities in themselves. They contain vending machines that sell gold, as well as artificial ski slopes, and giant aquariums.
- Accept any invitation to an *ifta* meal during Ramadan. People don't eat during the day during this religious festival, but they have a feast in the evening at sunset, D_____ .

Don't
- Visit in July or August, if at all possible. The weather is incredibly hot and humid, E_____ .
- Wear revealing clothing. Both men and women in the gulf wear long sleeves and cover their legs. The exception is at the city's beautiful beaches, F_____ .

C Cross out the extra word in each sentence.
1 My sister is always borrowing my clothes, which that gets on my nerves.
2 Nobody writes "dear" or even "hello" in emails any more, which I think it is really rude.
3 Kimchi, which I love it, is the spicy national dish of Korea.
4 The best time to visit my country is spring, when which it is warm and sunny.
5 The Lemon Tree Restaurant, which where we personally recommend, has amazing desserts.
6 Arriving late for class or meetings, which is common in my country, it is considered rude in Japan.

D Make it personal Complete the advice for your country.
1 The best time to visit my country is _____ , which _____ .
2 Our national dish is _____ , which _____ .
3 One thing to avoid in my country is _____ , which _____ .

What does your age group worry about most? 9.3

A It's a myth that only teenagers feel stressed by social media. People of all ages feel under tremendous pressure to keep up to date with Twitter, Facebook, and the rest. Thankfully, there are ways to reduce this level of stress.

B First of all, keep it small. Having lots of friends and followers gives you a massive egoboo (an 'ego boost') in the beginning, but it soon becomes difficult to keep responding to all those messages you receive from people you barely know. Only keep in contact with real friends online.

C Users on websites like Facebook create an image where everyone looks prosperous and happy. This makes people feel jealous of others. To avoid this, try not to compare your life to that of your friends and acquaintances online. Just use social media accounts to pass on updates about what's happening in your life.

D Many people also wrongly feel they should be connected to the workplace 24/7. With smartphones, workers can receive emails and WhatsApp messages even when they're not working. In your free time, close the programs and apps that your colleagues use, and don't look at them when you're not at work.

E Another problem in the workplace or at college is multitasking. In any modern classroom, the students have their tablets or laptops on while they listen to the lecturer. As well as taking notes, they check email, write reports, update Twitter, and peek at Facebook. This is too much for the brain to handle and encourages stress. To combat this, try to concentrate on just one task at a time to stop that feeling of a loss of control.

F You cannot control the Internet, but you can reduce the impact of the Internet and social media on your life. Just a few lifestyle changes can help reduce that feeling of stress, which can all too quickly take control of your life.

A Read the article. Choose the best title (1–3).
1 How to use the Internet efficiently at school and at work
2 How the Internet is changing our interests and behavior
3 How to stop teenagers worrying about the online world

B Match summary sentences 1–6 to the paragraphs (A–F).
1 People pretend their lives are perfect when they're on social media. ☐
2 Don't do too many things at once. ☐
3 It's not only young people who feel worried by the online world. ☐
4 Simple changes can make a big difference. ☐
5 It's impossible to stay in touch with everybody. ☐
6 Make sure you disconnect from your office when you're not there. ☐

C Circle the correct alternatives.
1 I *value / worth* my family and relations. They're incredibly important to me.
2 He has a different *appearance / outlook* to me on our career prospects. I'm positive about the future.
3 I couldn't care *less / more* about the changes at our college. They don't interest me at all.
4 People here are very *relaxed / tolerant* of others because there are so many different nationalities living and working together in the same place.
5 Are you *over / under* the impression that we have an exam tomorrow? It's not true if that's what you're thinking.
6 My dad and I don't see eye *to / with* eye about my career path. He wants me to be a lawyer, but I want to study drama.
7 I wasn't *awake / aware* of any disagreements between the teaching assistant and the students when I took the course last month.

D **Make it personal** Re-read 1–7 in C. Check (✓) the ones that sound most like something you've said or heard recently.

9.4 Would you be a good detective?

A ▶36 Listen to a news story. Then order the pictures 1–5.

B ▶36 Listen again and correct seven more factual errors in this summary of the crime.

A man broke into ~~an apartment~~ *a house* and committed a robbery in Miami. Unfortunately for him, he accidentally left his cell phone behind on a sofa. While the police were investigating the crime scene, his brother called his cell phone, and the police answered it. Not realizing who he was speaking to, he told the police his name because he wanted the phone back. The burglar denied committing the crime, saying that his phone had been lost. However, the police analyzed the messages on the phone and linked the man to four other crimes in the area.

C Reduce the relative clauses in sentences 1–7.
1 A man ~~who was~~ walking his dog witnessed the burglar leaving the property.
2 I get really annoyed at these companies who are calling my phone.
3 The man who was seen near the crime scene was wearing a red jacket.
4 Anyone who requires a special meal should reserve one online before the flight.
5 Books which are returned late to the library will incur a fine of 50 cents a day.
6 Only food that has been bought in the cafeteria may be eaten at these tables.
7 People who arrive late will not be admitted to the theater.

D Cross out the word which is different from the others in each group.
1 arrest burgle steal rob
2 burglar suspect robber thief
3 accept admit agree deny
4 rub scratch nod touch
5 invent comment lie make up
6 cheat allow litter speed

What do you spend the most money on? 9.5

A problem-solution essay

A Choose the correct alternatives to complete the essay.

What to do with all this clutter?

We are a nation of shopaholics. We buy more and more things that we don't need ¹*as / despite* more and more of our free time is spent in the mall. The problem comes when we take it all home. ²*Although / Unlike* people in the countryside, we city dwellers have no room in our small apartments for all these new purchases. Our homes are full of clutter.

Author Jen Hatmaker proposes an interesting solution. In her book *7: An experimental mutiny against excess*, Hatmaker says we should follow the rule of seven ³*because / in order to* reduce our spending. For example, she only wore seven items of clothing for a whole month ⁴*despite / so* that having a closet full of them. Even more surprisingly, she only ate seven types of food for a month, too.

⁵*As / Due to* the discovery that she had hundreds of pants, tops, and skirts that she didn't need, Hatmaker decided to clear out her closet. She gave these excess items away to charity ⁶*although / so that* other people could use them. Suddenly, she had no clutter.

⁷*Due to / While* most of us could only dream of having a closet like that, there are other simple ways of doing something similar. For example, you could cook the same seven meals each week ⁸*because / in order to* then you know exactly how much food to buy each time you go to the store.

⁹*Although / Unlike* Hatmaker's approach may seem too extreme for most people to follow, she does have powerful arguments for cutting down on all the clutter in our lives.

B T (true) or F (false)? We can infer that the author of the essay ...

1. is a shopaholic.
2. has a large house.
3. has hundreds of clothes.
4. doesn't often have enough money to eat well.
5. agrees with some, but not all, of Hatmaker's ideas.

C Correct the mistake in each sentence.

1. Not like my brother who speaks French and Chinese, I'm terrible at languages. _____
2. I wasn't able to go to the show due to have too much work. _____
3. You need to pass an English test in order to studying at a college in the U.S. _____
4. I'll upload the photos to the website so what everyone can see them. _____
5. Despite it was hot weather, they wouldn't put the air conditioning on. _____
6. We stopped for something to eat because of we had a few hours to wait for our flight.
_____

D Look back at lessons 9.1–9.5 in the Student's Book. Find the connection between the song lines and the content of each lesson.

E ▶ 37 Listen to the five question titles from the unit, and record your answers to them. If possible, compare recordings with a classmate.

10 » 10.1 How do you like to get around town?

A ▶38 Complete the conversation with the correct form of these phrasal verbs. Listen to check.

| dawn on | end up | get away | get through | look forward to | mix up |

EDDIE: I'm not ¹_____ going to dinner at my uncle's tomorrow. I don't know how I ²_____ the last one. It lasted for hours, and we ate more food at one lunch than I usually eat in a year.

IRIS: I know. It's impossible to ³_____. Once you're in the house, you're trapped!

EDDIE: And it only just ⁴_____ me on that we're supposed to bring the dessert, and now all the bakeries are closed. I'll probably ⁵_____ making one myself, and you know how bad my cooking is.

IRIS: Yes, please, anything but that! I still haven't recovered from the cake you made last year when you ⁶_____ the salt and the sugar.

EDDIE: Yeah, that was one of the worst. Well, I guess, you could cook if you like.

IRIS: No way. It's your family, Eddie – your cake!

B Correct the mistake in each sentence. One sentence is correct.
1. I'm not looking forward to go to the hospital tomorrow. _____
2. It only just dawned me on that we need a visa to go to the U.S. _____
3. That traffic jam was horrendous. Thank goodness, we finally got it through. _____
4. Some guy was painting graffiti right outside our apartment building, but he got away before the police arrived. _____
5. My dad always calls me by my sister's name, and vice-versa. He's always mixing up us. _____

C ▶39 Listen to Dave's travel nightmare story. Complete the summary.

Dave, who is a ¹_____, describes a terrible flight between ²_____ and ³_____. On the flight, a ⁴_____ suddenly became ill. Dave helped and as a reward, he was given ⁵_____ tickets to go ⁶_____ by the airline.

D ▶39 Listen again. T (true) or F (false)?
1. The other passenger was sitting across from Dave.
2. The man looked pale and was unable to speak.
3. The co-pilot whispered to Dave so nobody could hear them.
4. The man became ill towards the end of the flight.
5. When they landed, the doctor on the ground spoke the man's language.
6. The man made a complete recovery.

E Make it personal Complete the sentences so they're true for you.
1. The best way for a tourist to get around my hometown is _____.
2. To get around myself, I usually _____.
3. If I were really rich, my preferred form of transportation would be _____.
4. If I ran out of gas while driving near my home, I'd _____.

What's your idea of a perfect vacation? 10.2 «

A Complete 1–5 with the noun form of these phrasal verbs. There's one extra.

break down	check out	hand out	log in	mix up	rip off

1 I'm afraid there's been a _____ with your reservation. We'll need to arrange a room for you at another hotel.
2 They charged me $20 for a burger! It was a complete _____ .
3 We had a _____ on the highway. The car just stopped, and we couldn't start it again.
4 I can't use the hotel website because I don't have a _____ or a password.
5 What time is _____ tomorrow morning? Do I have to leave the hotel before midday?

B ⏵40 Circle the correct alternatives. Listen to check.

CHLOE: While I'm here in Colombia, I'd love to go to your famous mud baths. Could you tell me where ¹*they are / are they*?

PATY: The mud baths? That's my idea of a perfect vacation! Volcanic mud! It's so much fun! They're very near us here in Cartagena. The place is called El Totumo.

CHLOE: Do you know how long ²*it takes / does it take* to get there?

PATY: Not long. It's only 45 minutes from the city center.

CHLOE: Do you happen ³*know / to know* if they speak English there?

PATY: Yes, no problem. Lots of people speak English at the baths.

CHLOE: Oh, and I'd like to know ⁴*whether / which* I can bring my own food. We want to have a picnic.

PATY: That's fine. In fact, you have to bring your own food. There isn't a restaurant or café there.

CHLOE: One more thing. Can you check if ⁵*it is open / is it open* tomorrow?

PATY: Let me see. Just checking now. Er, yes, that's fine. It's open.

CHLOE: Wow, great! I'm going. One last thing: I wonder how ⁶*do I get / I get* the mud off afterwards.

PATY: That's the really fun part. You wash it off in the river next to the volcano!

CHLOE: No way!

PATY: Yes, absolutely. Everybody does it. You'll love it!

C Order the words to make questions.

1 is / like / summer / to / whether / know / I'd / in / your / country / very hot

_____

2 what time / you / me / could / most stores / tell / in / city / your capital / open / ?

_____

3 your / of / know / home / the name / a good restaurant / happen to / you / near / do / ?

_____

D **Make it personal** Answer the questions in **C** so they're true for you.

1 _____
2 _____
3 _____

49

10.3 Which foreign country would you most like to live in?

Reflections on my time in Japan
Elma Pereira

I went to Japan last year, and I fell in love with the country. Coming from São Paulo, it was a real culture shock at first, but it was also a homecoming for me. My grandparents emigrated to Brazil from Japan 50 years ago, and it was my first time going back to their homeland. I was discovering my **roots**. Now I'm thinking of studying there for a while.

The food was a real highlight for me. Everyone knows sushi, but I also loved the traditional noodles. You dip them into a kind of hot broth, which is like soup. They often come with bits of fish, which you **crumble** into soy sauce to make it tastier. There's nothing better on a frosty winter's day.

In Brazil, I'm studying fashion and I want to design clothes for a living. One of the great things about Tokyo's shops is that many sell beautiful fabrics. People buy these to make kimonos and other traditional garments. I bought so many samples from these shops, and they often don't even have a **label**. I'm now bursting with ideas for new designs.

Moving to Japan would be a big **leap** for me. One thing that will make the transition easier is that people are so friendly. People helped me out everywhere, and often spoke English, which was great because I could only say "arigato" and "sayonara" and you can't get far saying "thank you" and "good bye"!

I stayed at my cousins' house, which was a great way not only to save money – as accommodation and eating out are very expensive – but also to see how ordinary people live. Their apartment was very small, much smaller than ours back in Brazil, but it was brilliantly designed. Everything **fit** in a particular place, so you never noticed how small the living space actually was.

For me, the clothes in Japan are a **magnet** that draws me in and makes me want to learn more about the country. That's really why I want to live there, to learn how to capture the spirit of Japanese design.

A Read Elma's blog post. Check (✓) the things that she mentions.
☐ famous places ☐ clothes ☐ hotels ☐ meals ☐ parks ☐ the cost of living
☐ public transportation ☐ weather ☐ useful phrases ☐ people's homes ☐ the character of the people

B Re-read the blog. T (true) or F (false)?
1 Elma's parents originally come from Japan.
2 A broth is a liquid.
3 Elma is only interested in brand-name products.
4 She found it impossible to communicate with people.
5 She saw some relatives while she was in Tokyo.
6 She wants to get a job in Japan in the future.

C Do the words in bold in the blog have a literal (L) or figurative (F) meaning?
1 roots ☐ 2 crumble ☐ 3 label ☐ 4 leap ☐ 5 fit ☐ 6 magnet ☐

D Make it personal Complete the sentence so it's true for you.
I would / wouldn't like to live in Japan because _____.

Has your daily routine changed over time? 10.4

A ▶41 Complete the instant message conversation with these words. There's one extra. Listen to check.

| barely | culture clash | here and there | homesick | hustle and bustle | let alone | overwhelming |

Hey Sis!

Hi! How's your new life in Rome? 😊

Amazing! The ¹_____ of the city is great – I love getting lost in the crowds.

Cool! Do you miss home?

No, I don't feel ²_____ at all! Maybe it's because of all the history. It's quite ³_____ . People have been walking these streets for over 2,000 years!

Amazing! But what's everyday life like?

I've only had one ⁴_____ so far. There are no supermarkets in my local area, ⁵_____ a department store. That means I have to ask for products when I go shopping because everything is behind the counter.

Oh no! And you can ⁶_____ say anything more than "pizza" or "spaghetti" in Italian!

That's right! So as you can imagine, I've been eating a lot of pasta!

B Circle the correct alternatives.

My big life change ...

Francine Kelly, free climber

Q Francine, what was your big life change?
A About three years ago, I started free-climbing, that is, climbing without any ropes, just using my hands.

Q Why did you do that?
A I ¹*was / got* used to climbing with ropes because I had done it all my life and I wanted a new challenge.

Q Aren't you frightened of falling?
A ²*I get / I'm* used to heights so that's not a problem, but I still haven't ³*been / gotten* used to hanging off the side of a mountain with no ropes.

Q How did your life change when you started free-climbing?
A I needed a completely different routine. You need to prepare very carefully to go free-climbing even if you ⁴*are already / already get* used to a particular mountain.

Q What is your new routine?
A First of all, I climb the mountain in the normal way with ropes to ⁵*be / get* used to the route. At the same time, I "clean" the mountain. I remove any loose rocks or stones. It's difficult to find these rocks at first, but ⁶*I'm / I get* used to doing it now. When the mountain is clean, I repeat the climb without ropes.

Q How does your family feel about it?
A They hate it. My parents ⁷*cannot be / cannot get* used to the idea of me being on a mountain with no protection. However, they understand that it's my dream.

C Correct the mistake in each sentence. One sentence is correct.
1 Novak's working nights on his new job. He doesn't like it, but he's slowly used to it. _____
2 Living in Moscow is great, but we can't got used to cold weather. _____
3 Alexis was angry because the train was an hour late, but I'm used to train delays so it wasn't a problem for me. _____
4 I can't be used to being the project leader. I feel uncomfortable telling people what to do. _____
5 They say you get use to getting up at 5 a.m., but you never do. _____
6 If you need someone to drive the van for the trip, I can do it. I drive one for work, so I get used to it. _____

51

>> 10.5 Which are your two favorite cities and why?

A travel report

A Circle the correct alternatives (1–7) to complete the travel report below.

B ▶42 Re-read and complete paragraphs a–f with topic sentences 1–6. Listen to check.

1 Table Mountain sits above the city, and it's an iconic image of Cape Town.
2 If that wasn't enough, Cape Town also serves as a handy base for wildlife watching.
3 Cape Town is one of the most spectacular cities in the world, not just in South Africa.
4 By contrast, Robben Island is a tragic reminder of our country's difficult past.
5 The city has a Mediterranean climate, so it's pleasant to visit all year round.
6 Back at street level, you can explore the city's wide range of architectural styles.

The Cape of Good Times Alexandra Biko

a_____ I went there for the first time this year from my home town of Johannesburg, and it ¹*blew / broke* me away. Cape Town will ²*put / set* your imagination on fire.

b_____ It can be wet in winter and quite windy, too. The best time to visit is March through May, when the weather is perfect.

c_____ The views from the top were just ³*standing / stunning*. You can see both the city center with its famous harbor, as well as green slopes and the coast of the Atlantic Ocean. The ride there is epic, too. You take a cable car from the city center to the summit.

d_____ Start with a stroll around the old town. Many of the buildings here are over 300 years old, and they have a range of colonial styles. Nearby is Bo-Kaap, the Muslim District, with its ⁴*gorgeous / grateful* town houses and exotic spice shops.

e_____ It was the prison where many people were once incarcerated. Nelson Mandela was one of the most famous prisoners there. The story of his struggle is ⁵*awe-inspiring / good-looking*.

f_____ It's not really safari territory, but you can go to the whale coast, one of the best places in the world to see right whales. The sight of these amazing creatures will ⁶*put / take* your breath away, and it's just 115 kilometers from the city center.

Cape Town is magnificent. The culture, history, wildlife, and friendly people make it a trip of a lifetime. Watching dawn rise over Table Mountain is a sight that is magnificent ⁷*above / beyond* your wildest dreams. It's a perfect location for a vacation.

C **Make it personal** Imagine you want to visit Cape Town. Write a comment to post at the end of Alexandra's travel report. Include one question you could ask her.

_____

_____

D Look back at lessons 10.1–10.5 in the Student's Book. Find the connection between the song lines and the content of each lesson.

E ▶43 Listen to the five question titles from this unit, and record your answers to them. If possible, compare recordings with a classmate.

11 » 11.1 What recent news has caught your eye?

A ▶44 Listen and match the news stories 1–5 to the categories. There are two extra categories.

☐ Arts ☐ Crime ☐ Eating out ☐ Education ☐ Property ☐ Sports ☐ Unemployment

B ▶44 Listen again. Correct two pieces of false information in each summary.

News　Sport　Weather　Entertainment

1　~~Argentinian~~ *Brazilian* Paulo Orlando has become the first player from his country to play in the Baseball World Series. His team, the Kansas City Royals, lost the series against the New York Mets 4–1.

2　Some families in the U.S. are paid to live in empty homes. They don't have to clean it, but they do have to stay in the house because people are more likely to buy a property if someone lives there. The family members must always be at home when people come to see the property.

3　Mallie's Sports Bar and Grill in Northgate, Michigan, makes the world's largest burger. It weighs around 150 kilos, and you have to order it the day before you eat it.

4　The stars of Russia's Bolshoi Ballet are frequent visitors to Canada, and this year's tour features performances of the *Nutcracker* in Toronto and *Don Quixote* in Ottawa.

5　Oklahoma University Professor Kieran Mullen made headlines by destroying a laptop in front of his class. He picked up the machine from a desk and placed it in liquid oxygen, then dropped it on the floor where it broke into two halves. Fortunately, it was all a hoax designed to make his students concentrate on the class and not their computer screens.

C Complete the comments on a newspaper's website with these phrases.

| an accurate source　behind-the-scenes　biased　caught my eye　keep up with　skip |

1　Your sports correspondent is _____ against my team. He's always criticizing the New England Patriots. He doesn't have a good word to say about them.

2　It's easy for your newspaper to criticize the president, but you don't know what's happening _____ . She has access to information that none of your correspondents has.

3　It's crazy to use comments from a blogger to say that vaccinations are not safe. That blog was not _____ of information. It was written neither by a doctor nor a scientist.

4　I'm very disappointed you're no longer running reviews of Broadway plays. I subscribe to your paper just to _____ what's happening in the theater. Now, I'll be forced to look elsewhere.

5　A photo in your world news section _____ last weekend. Although the caption read that it was the Prime Minister of the Republic of Ireland, it was actually the country's President.

6　Like most people, I usually _____ the business pages, but I happened to read Maggie Bigelow's article on the Ivory Coast last weekend, and I found it fascinating. Congratulations!

D Make it personal Complete the sentences so they're true for you.

1　I don't read all of the news online. I usually skip _____ .

2　One website I always look at it is _____ to keep up with news about _____ .

3　The last photo that caught my eye was one of _____ .

53

11.2 Have you ever laughed at the wrong moment?

A Complete the phrases to describe being relaxed or nervous.

Have you ever laughed at the wrong moment?

Oh yes, absolutely, and my roommate, Rodrigo, was so angry – he completely ¹l_____ it. It all happened last year. Rodrigo was going away for the week, so I decided to earn a bit of extra money by renting out our apartment online to some tourists. I figured Rodrigo would be away so he would never see them. Boy oh boy, I was so wrong!

It was around the time when that volcano erupted here in Chile, and all flights were canceled. So without me knowing, Rodrigo had to come back to the apartment. He was in the shower when my guests, this family of four, entered the apartment. He completely ²f_____ out. Luckily, the family kept their ³c_____ . The mother called my cell phone, and I explained the mix-up.

I asked her to stay ⁴c_____ and pass the phone to Rodrigo. He was still in the living room in his robe! Well, I couldn't keep it ⁵t_____ any longer, and I just started to laugh. He went ballistic. Not surprisingly, we stopped sharing a place soon after that! Oh, and the family never paid me a cent, either, as they ended up staying at a hotel.

B Report sentences 1–6 from the story. Remember to move the verb one tense back.

1 "There are some strangers in our apartment!"
   Rodrigo said _____.
2 "No flights were able to leave today because of the volcano."
   Rodrigo said _____.
3 "We booked the apartment online."
   The mother said _____.
4 "We can always stay at a hotel."
   The father said _____.
5 "I'll never forgive you for this!"
   Rodrigo said _____.
6 "I'm really, really sorry, Rodrigo."
   I told Rodrigo _____.

C Put the words in order to complete the reported questions.

1 (there / they / doing / were / what) Rodrigo asked the family _____.
2 (I / when / back / was / coming) Rodrigo asked _____.
3 (mistake / whether / a / there / had / been) The mother asked _____.
4 (go / would / where / they) We asked the family _____.

What was the last video you shared? 11.3

A ▶ 45 Read the article and put the paragraphs A–E in order 1–5. Listen to check.

The Dancing Traffic Light Manikin

A ☐ By waiting and watching the movements of this figure, these people aren't trying to rush across the road. As the video says, pedestrian crossings are the most dangerous place for traffic accidents in cities. By contrast, the green figure just stands still. Otherwise people would watch it dancing, too!

B ☐ This is what led to its huge viral success. It has, count them, over 115 million views on YouTube. In addition, 81% more people waited at the light, avoiding any possibility of accidents. That's something to be proud of.

C [1] People falling over, cats in hats, celebrity jokes: there are lots of reasons why a video might go viral, but surely the best of all is because it saves lives. That was the case in the 2014 hit *The Dancing Traffic Light Manikin* by Smart.

D ☐ Haven't seen it? The idea is simple. Pedestrians wait at a busy pedestrian crossing. The red figure tells them to stop, but instead of standing in one place, it starts to dance in lots of different ways. The people waiting start laughing, and watch the red figure dancing until the end.

E ☐ But just waiting at the traffic light wouldn't make the video go viral: there's also a catch. The dancing traffic light isn't pre-programmed. It imitates live dancing by members of the public. People go into a special booth where a camera records their dance steps. These are then copied by the red figure on the traffic light.

B Re-read. T (true), F (false) or NI (no information)? Have you seen the video? If not, search for it online.
1 The Dancing Light Manikin was set up in lots of different cities.
2 The objective of the video was to encourage public safety.
3 81% of all pedestrians waited to watch the video.
4 Almost all viral videos are funny ones.
5 Only the red figure moves in the traffic light.
6 The red man copies the movements of professional dancers.

C Match 1–6 to responses a–f.
1 I didn't know that most road accidents happen at pedestrian crossings.
2 I saw a video of a grandfather seeing his grandson for the first time after 25 years.
3 This hip-hop video is so cool. I've been dancing to it all week.
4 I can't believe you were on the news. I thought you were far too shy to talk to a reporter.
5 Did you see that video of the wedding group on a bridge, where the bridge breaks and they all fall into the water?
6 I really hate videos where people are cruel to animals.

a ☐ I agree. That gets to me, too.
b ☐ Really? It does nothing for me.
c ☐ Me too. It moved me to tears.
d ☐ No. That got me thinking, too.
e ☐ Oh yeah! I burst out laughing.
f ☐ What can I say? They caught me by surprise.

11.4 What's your definition of gossip?

A ▶46 Complete the conversations with these phrases. Listen to check.

| between you and me | didn't tell a soul | have my word | keep it to yourself |
| me and my big mouth | my lips are sealed | never guess | spread it around |

Conversation 1

A: There's only one way that Karen found out about the surprise party. You told her.
B: No! I swear! I ¹_____!
A: Well, anyway, she knows now. Just don't tell Daisy too, all right?
B: She won't hear about it from me. ²_____.
A: She'd better not. I'm just worried that Mike is going to ³_____. That guy can't keep a secret to save his life.
B: Trust me, OK. He won't say anything. You ⁴_____.
A: You'd better be right!

Conversation 2

C: I heard that your brother was caught cheating on an exam.
D: Yes, well, no one else knows, so ⁵_____, OK?
C: Oh! I told Nigel, too.
D: What?
C: ⁶_____. I'm so sorry. We were talking about the exam, and it slipped out.
D: Well, please, please don't tell anyone else.
C: OK but, ⁷_____, he wasn't the only one they caught cheating. You'll ⁸_____ who else was caught. Michael Parker!
D: No way!
C: Yes! Ah, you like hearing about secrets now.

B Correct the mistake in each sentence. One sentence is correct.

1 The doctor urged me do more exercise for the sake of my health. _____
2 They agreed no to tell anyone the news until Monday. _____
3 Bill promised help me find a job as soon as possible. _____
4 My parents persuaded me go to college. I didn't want to go. _____
5 They threatened throwing us off the train if we didn't show them our tickets. _____
6 Hugo's parents begged him not to join the fire department because they thought it was too dangerous. _____
7 The hotel refused refund my money even though I showed them that I had overpaid. _____
8 I wanted to talk about our Internet site in the meeting, but they wouldn't let me to change the subject. _____

C Choose the correct alternatives. Have you ever played *Telephone*? What's it called in your language?

We've all played the game *Telephone*. In this simple game, you stand in line. The person at one end thinks of a sentence. He or she whispers it in a neighbor's ear and tells that person ¹*repeat / to repeat* the sentence to a neighbor, and so on until everyone has heard and repeated it. Everyone then compares the final sentence with the original to see whether or not it's the same. The person who came up with the sentence has to promise ²*not to tell / to not tell* it to anyone until the end.

In 2012, an Australian man called Philip Minchin persuaded people all around the world ³*joining / to join* a global game of *Telephone*. People in libraries all over the world agreed ⁴*to play / play*. They even let people ⁵*take part / to take part* whose first language wasn't English. It began in Melbourne, Australia as "Life must be lived as play," a quotation from the Greek Philosopher Plato. The message then moved across six continents until it reached Alaska, in the U.S. And the final message? Nobody expected ⁶*hearing / to hear* the same sentence, but what was repeated was completely bizarre: "He bites snails!"

Would you enjoy being world-famous? 11.5 «

A letter of complaint

A Read the email and check (✓) the four items that Silvio complains about.

1 ☐ the availability of seats   3 ☐ his luggage   5 ☐ the staff
2 ☐ the in-flight menu   4 ☐ the company website   6 ☐ the cost of the tickets

---

To: customerservices@flyways.net

From: sbacelli@mymail.net

Subject: Complaint

Dear Sir / Madam

I am writing to you in ^{1}r__ g__ __ __ to my experience on flight XL923 with your airline on August 9th. I had booked three seats on this flight for myself and my parents. Our experience was extremely unsatisfactory, so I am writing to complain.

First of all, our flight was overbooked, and only two people were allowed to board. We were obviously unwilling to split our group, so we were all forced to wait for the next flight. This overbooking took place despite the fact that we had previously reserved seats online.

It is my ^{2}b__ __ __ __f that we are entitled to compensation as a result of the long wait in the airport, during which we were only given a $5 voucher for some sandwiches.

To make ^{3}m__ __t __ __s worse, before we boarded the later flight, we were asked to place our bags in the hold. Your unsympathetic staff insisted very forcefully that our bags were too large to go in the overhead compartments in the cabin. Your website claims that passengers are permitted to carry bags of 25x45x56 centimeters on all flights. In ^{4}r__ __ l__ __y, bags of that size are only permitted for business class customers. Your website is misleading.

I would also like to ^{5}c__ __ __ your attention to the government guidelines for fair treatment of passengers. Following the information given there, I believe that we are entitled to a refund on the price of our tickets for this flight.

Sincerely

Silvio Bacelli

B Complete the missing letters in the phrases for writing a letter or email of complaint.

C Silvio also ordered a special vegetarian meal for the flight. This was forgotten, and he was only offered a standard meal. Add this complaint to his email.

_____

_____

D Look back at lessons 11.1–11.5 in the Student's Book. Find the connection between the song lines and the content of each lesson.

E ⦾47 Listen to the five question titles from the unit, and record your answers to them. If possible, compare recordings with a classmate.

57

12 » 12.1 How optimistic are you?

A ▶48 Read the podcast title. Guess if the speakers will agree (A) or disagree (D) with these statements. Listen to check your ideas.

1 Optimists often make mistakes with money.
2 Pessimists make bad employees.
3 Pessimists are better at planning than optimists.
4 Optimists are healthier people than pessimists.
5 Pessimists tend to take lots of safety precautions.

> **Today on the podcast:** "It's not all bad" - why a little bit of pessimism can be good for you, with Jenna Doyle and Keith Woods.

B ▶48 Listen again and complete the summary with words you hear on the podcast.

> People think pessimism is bad, a destructive form of ¹_____ , but, in fact, it can be a good thing. Optimists often ²_____ a lot of money because they are sure that they can pay it back, which is not always true.
>
> Pessimists are also more effective in the workplace. Although people are expected to be positive in ³_____ , in working life, pessimists are better because they make better ⁴_____ for the future.
>
> Surprisingly, ⁵_____ doctors have found that pessimism is also good for health. Pessimists go to the doctor as soon as possible, whereas optimists often ⁶_____ medical problems until it's too late. In the same way, pessimists are less likely to be injured in accidents because they take ⁷_____ precautions like wearing a helmet on a bike.
>
> Being a pessimist is not ⁸_____ - there are benefits to looking on the bad side of life.

C Complete the conversations with these words. There are two extras.

best	better	bright	dream	good	safe	tunnel	wishful

1 A: I have my lottery ticket, and we're going to be millionaires on Friday!
   B: Yeah, _____ on!
2 A: I went for a job interview on Monday, and they still haven't gotten back to me.
   B: Don't worry. No news is _____ news.
3 A: If we hang around outside the movie opening, we might get to take a selfie with one of the stars.
   B: Come on, Lucas, that's just _____ thinking.
4 A: Do we really need to take all these medicines with us on vacation? Your suitcase is like a pharmacy!
   B: Better _____ than sorry.
5 A: I'm worrying it might rain over the weekend, and we're having a barbecue.
   B: Yes, but it also might not. You have to hope for the _____ .
6 A: How frustrating! The office computer system is down. I can't do anything.
   B: Well, look on the _____ side; we can probably go home early today.

What will the world be like in 100 years? 12.2

A Can you imagine a 3D phone? Read the article and circle the correct alternatives.

The 3D phone is coming

What will future phone calls be like?

Forget video calls. All of us will soon ¹*have made / be making* 3D calls all day, every day. Polish company Leia Display Systems is already building a prototype which will ²*be completely finishing / have completely finished* by the end of next year. *Star Wars* fans will ³*have already recognized / already be recognizing* that the company is named after Princess Leia, who sends a 3D hologram of herself in *Star Wars*.

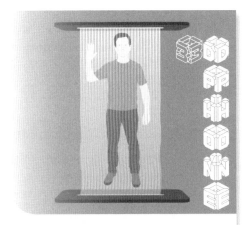

How will the 3D phone ⁴*work / be working*?

To send calls, users will ⁵*sit / have sat* in front of a special camera, which records their image and sends it to the recipient. Then a laser projects the caller's image onto water vapor, which creates a 3D image of them. Users ⁶*will need / be needing* a large room to receive calls because the image is life-size. The developers ⁷*have worked / will be working* on a smaller version once the original goes on sale.

Who's the 3D phone for?

Although most of us will ⁸*continue / have continued* to use our traditional smartphones, the 3D version has some particularly useful applications. In the first few years, people will probably ⁹*be using / have used* it for acting auditions, or in the fashion industry to see how clothes look on models. This ¹⁰*will be saving / is going to save* thousands of dollars in plane fares if customers can appear to be in the same room even if they are actually hundreds of miles away.

B Rewrite the sentences using the word in CAPITALS. Do not change the word.

1 We're going to finish our project before March 4th. HAVE
   We'll have finished our project by March 4th.

2 The population will certainly keep growing. BOUND

3 This time tomorrow, we're going to be sitting on a beach in Acapulco. WILL

4 Everyone will leave before midnight, I promise you. LEFT

5 In 2050, people will be living on the surface of Mars. ARE

6 Barcelona FC will probably win the League next year. LIKELY

C Put *by* in the correct place or places in these sentences.

1 *Hamlet*, which was written Shakespeare in about 1599, remains his best-known play.

2 This cake was made me and my mom – do you want some?

3 We walked here, but are getting home taxi as we have to be home midnight.

4 Bus fares have gone up 10% in the last year and trains even more!

12.3 What's the coldest place you've ever been to?

A Read the article and answer the questions.
1 Where is Oymyakon?
2 What was the coldest ever temperature recorded there?
3 How can you translate "Oymyakon" into English?
4 When do public buildings close in Oymyakon?
5 How long does it take to get there from the airport?

The coldest town in the world ... gets even colder!

Temperatures in Oymyakon fell to new lows last night as winter gripped this town in north-western Russia. The mercury dropped to an incredible −71 Centigrade, the lowest figure ever recorded for a populated area.

Set in one of the most hostile environments imaginable and originally a stopover point for farmers to sell their reindeer, farmers were attracted to the town's hot springs, giving Oymyakon its surprising name – it means something like "the water that doesn't freeze."

Winter is inevitably a long, hard time for local residents to endure. Coupled with the problems of ice and snow, there are also frequent communication breakdowns; it's so cold cell phones won't work!

As long-distance travel gets easier, you'd expect residents to leave for places with warmer weather, but it seems locals are used to their tough environment. Life carries on as normally as possible. For example, the local school will remain open as long as it's warmer than −50 Centigrade outside!

Other temperature-related issues Oymyakonians have to deal with include leaving their cars running when not in use because that way they are bound to start when they need them. Sometimes once the engine is turned off, vehicles never work again.

As the world's temperatures get ever more extreme, who knows what the future holds for this desolate community? Perhaps ever more curious visitors will want to explore this northern region where no crops grow, and the only industry is cutting wood. Without a doubt, anyone brave enough to pay Oymyakon a call will be a true adventurer. It is only accessible by snow-covered roads, a two-day trip from the nearest airport at Yakutsk. That's if the planes are running, of course. Feeling brave? Come visit Oymyakon!

B Check (✓) the statements the writer is certain about.
1 Oymyakon is the most hostile urban environment in the world.
2 Cell phones cannot function in Oymyakon in winter.
3 Residents leave their engines running to be sure that the car won't break down.
4 The new low temperatures will bring lots of new tourists to the town.
5 Oymyakon is a tourist destination only for the adventurous.

C Complete the phrases in these exchanges.
1 A: Do you think Dirk will be able to complete the marathon?
   B: I h_____ my d_____ . He's not in great shape, but you never know.
2 A: Wow, that skateboarding trick was amazing! I've caught it on camera.
   B: I know. I can't believe I p_____ it o_____ ! I've never been able to do it before!
3 A: We have five guests staying tonight, but only two bedrooms. I don't know what to do.
   B: Don't worry. We'll f_____ o_____ a way to fit everyone in.
4 A: Something's wrong with my laptop. The screen keeps switching off. Any idea why?
   B: Sorry, I don't h_____ a c_____ . Guess you need to get it to an expert.
5 A: Have you heard about this new virus? What are they saying in the papers?
   B: They say it could p_____ a t_____ to people throughout the region.

What was the last excuse you made?   12.4 «

A Circle the correct alternatives.

1 A: Could you tell me what time the ferry is?

B: *It always leaves / It's always leaving* at 8 a.m., and then *it comes back / it's coming* back at 5.30 p.m. every day.

2 A: Do you know what you are doing over the weekend?

B: Not sure. I guess *I'll watch / I'm watching* a movie, but I have no idea, really.

3 A: These bags are really heavy. I can't carry them on my own.

B: Really? Wait there! *I'm helping / I'll help* you.

4 A: George! I think *it's raining / it's going to rain*. Can you bring the laundry in, please?

B: What? It's OK. There aren't any clouds out there. Let's leave the clothes out.

5 A: I really need someone to help me move this evening.

B: Really? I *don't do / I'm not doing* anything this evening. I can help.

6 A: Who do you think *will win / is winning* the game tomorrow?

B: The Minnesota Timberwolves! They're the best basketball team around.

B ▶49 Complete the conversation with a future form of the verbs in parentheses. Sometimes more than one form is possible. Listen to hear the most common forms.

BETH: Hey, Charlie, What time ¹_____ (we / meet) for the party tonight?

CHARLIE: I don't know, Beth. Actually ... I can't come.

BETH: What? Everyone thinks you ²_____ (come)! What's the problem?

CHARLIE: I have a black eye. A real shiner. It's ridiculous. I banged my head on a sign in my local bus station, and it swung back and hit me in the eye. I ³_____ (write) an email to complain. I'm just thinking about what to say.

BETH: Come on, it's only a black eye. Yes, it's embarrassing, but you got it in an accident. You can't hide at home. Anyway, Milan ⁴_____ (bring) a cake for you. He made it this morning, and it looks amazing.

CHARLIE: I'm sorry. I ... I ⁵_____ (call) Milan to apologize, OK? I just can't go out. I've already decided. I ⁶_____ (stay) at home.

BETH: Look ... I know. I ⁷_____ (come) to your house and have a look. I'm sure it's not as bad as you think. Then we ⁸_____ (go) to the party together. You ⁹_____ (feel) better if you go there with someone else.

CHARLIE: Really? Well, OK, thanks, Beth. You're so kind. But promise you won't laugh, OK?

C Correct the mistake in each sentence. One sentence is correct.

1 I won't go out until your package will arrive, OK? _____

2 I'm going to visit the Prado Museum before I'll leave Madrid. _____

3 We're staying at home until it stops snowing. _____

4 After you will meet Joe, come and see me, please. _____

5 Dana tells you the time of our train as soon as she knows it. _____

6 When I'll get paid, I'll give you back the $100 I owe you. _____

D Make it personal What's the worst excuse you have ever heard? Why did the person make the excuse?

_____

_____

61

>> 12.5 What will your life be like 10 years from now?

A Read Antonia's email to her future self and circle the correct alternatives.

Hello Antonia!

1 How are you? I do hope you're well! This is my email to myself to read at the end of our English course here in Boston! ¹*Hopefully / Officially*, you'll speak much better English when you read this and be able to spot and correct any errors you've made! It's the first day today, and you're going to learn a lot over the next year.

2 My first piece of advice is to keep in touch with everyone you've met in the course. You've ²*officially / finally* gotten the chance to meet people from all around the world, and you should ³*definitely / inevitably* try to stay in touch with as many of them as possible. You may even get the chance to visit them.

3 Secondly, I'd encourage you to take a recognized exam in English now. This is ⁴*certainly / finally* the best time to do so because you'll have been studying English a lot over the last eight months, and you may never reach the same level again. It's essential to get a document that ⁵*officially / probably* shows your English level, for future employers, for example.

4 After the course and the exams, you're ⁶*hopefully / inevitably* going to forget a lot of what you've learned, unless you keep working on your English at home. You should read an article that interests you online every day, listen to as much English as possible, and keep chatting with your ex-classmates, too. That way you'll ⁷*eventually / officially* get used to "thinking" in English as a daily habit.

5 I imagine you're ⁸*definitely / probably* feeling pretty down now at the thought of leaving the U.S. and all your new friends, but try to think positively. Nothing lasts forever, and you've had a great opportunity that many people never get to enjoy.

Have a safe trip home and bye from the past!

Antonia

B Re-read and match paragraphs 1–5 to the information they contain. There's one extra.

- [ ] further practice after the course
- [ ] the most important lesson
- [ ] English is important for your career
- [ ] use it as an opportunity to travel
- [ ] when the email was written
- [ ] look on the bright side

C **Make it personal** Look back at a piece of writing you did earlier in the course. What errors can you find? How could you improve it?

D Look back at lessons 12.1–12.5 in the Student's Book. Find the connection between the song lines and the content of each lesson.

E ▶50 Listen to the five question titles from the unit, and record your answers to them. If possible, compare recordings with a classmate.

62

Selected audio scripts

3 page 6 exercises A and B

J = Jackie, K = Ki-Yeon

J: What are those, Ki-Yeon?
K: What?
J: These wooden birds.
K: Oh, they're wooden ducks. In Korea, it's traditional to give wooden ducks like these as a wedding gift. They're a present from my future mother-in-law, Soo.
J: They're really cute.
K: Yeah. Soo's such a lovely lady. She'll be the perfect mother-in-law.
J: So, how are the preparations going? It's hard to organize a wedding, isn't it?
K: Hard? It's a nightmare. Do you have any difficult people in your family?
J: I only have difficult people in my family! What's the problem?
K: We want to have a traditional Korean wedding, OK? So usually the parents pay for the wedding. Each family pays half the money.
J: So?
K: David, my stepfather, doesn't want to pay. He thinks it's too expensive. It's no use discussing it with him. He refuses to pay his half.
J: Oh no!
K: And that's not all. I asked my brother, Pete, well, my half-brother, to prepare the wedding invitations.
J: Uh-huh.
K: He hasn't done it yet. Pete hasn't sent any wedding invitations to anyone. He's always like this. It's impossible for him to do anything quickly!
J: When is the wedding?
K: In July.
J: And it's now February.
K: Right. We don't have a lot of time.
J: Any other problems?
K: The food! My cousin runs a restaurant and she agreed to provide the catering.
J: Well, that's one problem solved.
K: No, it's not. She's now expecting a baby on the day of the wedding!
J: Maybe a new caterer would be better. Is anyone else in your family helping you?
K: Hmm ... My aunt, Min-Jun. She wants to help, so she calls me all the time. Yesterday, she asked me about the flowers for the ceremony, and the phone call took an hour! An hour!
J: OK, OK. Keep calm. Look, Ki-Yeon, you can't arrange this wedding on your own. It's essential for you to get some help. Talk to your friends. Ask them to help you because you have an awful lot of things to do over the next few months!
K: Tell me about it!

6 page 11 exercises A and B

F = Frank Mortimer, R = Rachel Schultz, A = Dr Alba Lopez

F: It all began in March 1995 in Puerto Rico. A farmer discovered eight sheep in a field with all their blood missing. This was the first recorded case of the chupacabra, the goat-sucker, a mysterious monster that drinks the blood of animals. Welcome to *Science Fiction or Science Fact?* I'm Frank Mortimer. I'm here with author and journalist, Rachel Schultz. She investigates animals that may or may not exist. Rachel, hello.
R: Hi Frank.
F: So, tell us, what does the chupacabra look like?
R: Well, eyewitnesses say that the chupacabra is a big gray animal with red eyes. It moves like a kangaroo and it has spines on its back.
F: You can't be serious!
R: Many different witnesses have seen the animal. They all give the same description. I'm pretty sure they're telling the truth.
F: I doubt that, but OK. And, where have people seen the chupacabra?
R: Since the first sighting in 1995, there have been reports of chupacabras in Puerto Rico, the continental United States, Mexico, and Chile.
F: Chile too? So, not just North America. Hmm. Does it attack people?
R: No, all the records show attacks on animals such as goats, ...
F: Obviously.
R: Dogs, and cows.
F: Rachel, thank you. Now, I think we have Dr Alba Lopez on the line, a biologist from Puerto Rico. Alba?
A: Hello? Hello?
F: Alba, hi, it's Frank here on *Science Fiction or Science Fact?* Can you hear me?
A: Yes, I can.
F: Dr Alba Lopez, you're a biologist. The chupacabra doesn't really exist, does it? I mean, anything might have killed those animals.
A: I really doubt that there's a blood-sucking monster with red eyes out there!
F: So, how do you explain the stories of the chupacabra?
A: Well, something must have killed these animals, that's for sure. I think it might have been a coyote.
F: A coyote? A wild dog? How do you explain that?
A: The coyote might have been ill. When they're ill, coyotes can become thin and gray, like descriptions of the chupacabra. And coyotes kill and eat farm animals all the time.
F: Rachel, your thoughts?
R: It can't have been a coyote. These farmers know about animals. It might have been an animal unknown to science.
F: Well, there we have it. A new, mystery animal or a sick coyote. Rachel, Alba, thank you both. So, what do you think? If you want to get in on the debate, log onto our website and leave a comment. We look forward to hearing your thoughts.

11 page 16 exercises A and B

Conversation 1

I = Interviewer, R = Ron

I: What was your favorite activity as a child, Ron?
R: Er ... let me think. Um, well, when I was about 13, I loved role-playing games.
I: Role-playing games? Like Dungeons and Dragons?
R: Yeah, you know, you imagine you're a hero or a wizard and you have all kinds of adventures with your friends. You get these big rule books and you also need dice to play. It was pretty complicated.
I: Did you use to dress up? Wear special costumes or masks?
R: No! We didn't use to wear any special clothes. It was all about using your imagination. We used to play on the dining table at home. We'd always get some nachos and sodas and we would play for hours.
I: Did lots of people use to do this?
R: Absolutely! It was a huge fad back in the 1980s. Remember, we didn't have cell phones, X boxes or the internet, so we had to create our own fantasies much more.
I: Of course! Different times. And, do you still play these games?
R: Hmm, well I used to play them in college but I stopped many years ago. I have a son and a daughter now and when they're a bit older I might introduce them to the games. Why not? They're a lot of fun. If I can get them away from their phones, of course.

Conversation 2

I = Interviewer, M = Mary

I: What was your favorite activity as a child, Mary?
M: When I was 12, roller-blading was a huge fad. I used to love it!
I: I had a pair of skates once too! Loved them. Where did you use to go roller-blading?
M: My dad would take me to the park. Sometimes I'd go rollerblading with my friends too. Everyone had rollerblades back then. We used to love them.
I: How did you get into it?
M: Well, my best friend had a pair of rollerblades and I thought they were so cool. I used to talk about them all the time and so my parents bought me a pair for my twelfth

Selected audio scripts

birthday. They were black and so was my helmet. I still have them today actually, stored away somewhere. Even though they don't fit any more, I just can't seem to throw them away.

I: Really? Do you still go roller-blading these days?

M: Sadly not. I had an accident once when I was about 14. Horrible! I was skating along a bike path, hit a stone, fell and broke my leg! I couldn't walk for a whole summer. It was just awful, scary too, and it turned me off roller-blading after that.

▶ 16 *page 21 exercises A, B and C*

L = Luisa, J = Jacques

L: I was on a flight the other day from New York to L.A. and there was a woman next to me who was traveling by herself. She looked familiar and then my husband said, you two look like each other. And it was true. We both had long straight hair and brown eyes. We took a selfie to prove it. It was weird. That's what has inspired my big question today. Do we all have a double? Jacques?

J: It's very likely, Luisa. There isn't an infinite number of genes. In a population of millions, it's very possible that someone will look like you. I myself look a lot like a good friend. People often think we're brothers.

L: Uh-huh. People often look like family members. That's natural but we're talking about strangers who look like one another.

J: What is a stranger? Many people share a common ancestor. For example, 1 in every 200 men alive today is a descendant of Genghis Khan. Genghis Khan was the emperor of Mongolia and he died in 1227. So if you do the math, he by himself is a direct ancestor of an enormous number of people alive today.

L: Is it possible that we have *more* than one double?

J: We like to have a very special image of ourselves. We're all individuals. In fact, some experts believe we may each have seven lookalikes in the world.

L: How can people prove it?

J: I don't know about "prove it" but there are websites out there. One is TwinStrangers. net.

L: How does it work?

J: You choose drawings that describe yourself. You then compare the details with the information from other users on the site. If someone has a similar description, you look at the photos and see if you have found your lookalike.

L: Is it free?

J: No, you pay to use the site, but there is a Facebook group too.

L: Amazing, I might try it myself.

▶ 18 & 19 *page 23 exercises A, B and C*

Golden Globe Award-winning actor Peter Dinklage has achieved unbelievable success. However, like many actors, he had to overcome extreme poverty at the beginning of his career. Moreover, as a "dwarf" (properly known as a "little person" today), Dinklage faced many difficulties in finding decent parts to play. In fact, he had to say "no" to many early roles in order to pursue his dream of becoming a serious actor.

Dinklage was born in New Jersey in 1969. He wasn't from an acting family at all. His dad was a salesperson and his mom was a teacher, but Dinklage loved theater from an early age. He was in 5th grade when he heard his first big round of applause in a school play.

Eager to start an acting career, Dinklage moved to New York City in 1991 and it was there that his problems began.

Dinklage has dwarfism, which means his adult height is around 1.27 meters. There are plenty of roles for actors of that size, but Dinklage refused to take them. He didn't want to play magical creatures like elves in ads and children's movies. He preferred to wait for appropriate roles, which meant he often starved. He lived in a small apartment, where he could hear the trains going by. The apartment also had rats. Dinklage says he sometimes paid for his dinner in dimes – 10 cent pieces – because he had no other money. Fortunately, his career slowly took off. In 2003, he starred in the movie *The Station Agent* which was an independent hit. Finally people were noticing Dinklage for his talent.

Then everything changed when he became one of the stars of the fantasy series *Game of Thrones* in 2011. His performance was incredible, and it won him a Golden Globe at the age of 42. Finally Dinklage had triumphed. And the biggest decision of his life had been saying "no" to all those terrible roles in the past.

▶ 22 *page 28 exercises B, C and D*

P = Presenter, I = Isabelle Sharpe

P: And now over to Isabella Sharpe, our new "tech tips" specialist.

I: Hello. What's the first website you look at in the morning? What's your home page? What's your first stop to finding out anything? For most people, the answer is probably Google. But, is Google the only search engine in town? Certainly not. It's just one of a range of possible websites you can use. So, what alternatives are there? Let's look at three of them.

Perhaps the competitor to Google that most people have heard of is Microsoft's Bing. To look up information, it works in a very similar way to Google. Some people suggest that Google is still slightly better than Bing at some searches, but they aren't so different.

DuckDuckGo is an indie. It's a search engine from a small start-up, and much less well-known. It's just as good but, unlike Google, DuckDuckGo does not track your movements online. The fact that it records user data is a serious drawback of using Google. If you are searching for something and you want to keep it a secret, like a new job when you're in the office, DuckDuckGo is a risk-free alternative.

Finally, there's CCSearch. Now they say that they are not a search engine but the program works very much like one. CCSearch helps you find images and content that you can use for free. Perhaps you are self-publishing a book and you need some photos, but you don't have any money. CCSearch will find free photos for you to use. However, you may still have to pay third parties for these images. Be aware that you use the site at your own risk.

Whichever way you look at it, Google has set the standard for search engines and continues to lead the pack. It's easy-to-use interface, along with its rapid, efficient search results, meant it really does deserve its place at the summit. Having said that, nothing lasts forever, and the younger competitors are starting to want a piece of the action.

That's all for now. I'm Isabella Sharpe. Thank you so much for listening.

▶ 28 *page 36 exercises A and B*

J = James Thompson, Y = Adriana Ritchie

J: Adriana, when was the last time you heard kids complaining in an art gallery because they couldn't see enough art?

A: I've never ever heard of that.

J: Don't frown. This really happened.

A: I don't believe you, James. Kids get bored in museums.

J: It happened at the Tate Modern, London's biggest Modern Art gallery.

A: Modern Art? I don't understand that. I spend all my time squinting at the pictures, and I still can't figure out what they are.

J: Tate Modern isn't just about paintings. The museum used to be a power station. Its entrance hall is enormous, and they put giant artworks there. I saw a slide by the Belgian artist Carsten Höller.

A: So the kids were complaining because they couldn't go on the slide?

J: That's right. One of the kids had tickets for the slide, and the others didn't.

A: Uh-oh!

J: It was OK. I had some spare tickets, and I gave them to the kids. We can't let kids miss their favorite art, can we?

A: I'm nodding, listeners, I'm nodding. So how was the slide?

J: It was fun, but it was over in about five seconds. You also had to wear knee pads and elbow pads.

A: What, like on a skateboard? Was it dangerous?

J: No! They were just being careful. Anyway, I wanted another try at it, but the other people with me wanted to see the rest of the gallery, so there wasn't time.

A: OK. I'm scratching my head here, James. How is this slide art?

J: Höller believes that slides are interesting because you lose control on the slide, and you feel really happy afterwards.

A: That's fun, not art.

J: When kids paint, they make art and they have fun.

A: I don't think it's art.

J: Höller also says the slide is an interesting shape. It's round. It has curves. Most

64

Selected audio scripts

of our modern buildings are square, or rectangular. The slide is a different shape. It's another way of looking at the world.

A: Ah, now I understand!

J: You see. Art is for everyone.

A: Can I still see this artwork at the Tate Modern?

J: Sorry, Adriana. It was only a temporary exhibition. Höller's slides have appeared in some other galleries, in Germany and the U.S., so maybe you will see another one somewhere else in the future.

▶ 31 page 39 exercises A and B

L = Luca, M = Martina

L: Wow! Love the photo, Martina. What a stunning island! Where on earth ...?

M: That, Luca, is Niihau Island in Hawaii.

L: Niihau. I thought that meant Hello in Chinese!

M: Not Nihao. Niihau.

L: Sorry. I've never heard of it!

M: That's because it's one of the most difficult places in the world to visit. For many years, tourists couldn't go to Niihau at all.

L: Why?

M: It's a private island with just a few villages. The owner made the rules. In the past you could only go there if you lived there.

L: But now anyone can go there? Er, are you telling me you were able to visit this place?

M: Uh-huh. Only a few tourists can get in every year. I managed to go there by helicopter with my parents. It was amazing.

L: Lucky you! What's it like? I mean, were you able to meet any of the locals?

M: Yes, one or two. Everyone speaks English. They were very friendly and seemed extremely happy to live in their simple, beautiful island paradise.

L: Awesome! Could you stay the night there?

M: No, our limit was three hours! But at least we were able to go snorkeling. I saw some amazing fish. The sea is crystal clear. And so warm, like the perfect bath! And the beaches are the most wonderful white sand, like walking on warm snow! And ...

L: Stop! I hate you! Did you see any whales or dolphins?

M: No, that's about the only thing we didn't see.

L: Well, I saw a whale once in Mexico. Briefly. Just for a few seconds. I was just able to take a photo before it disappeared under the water.

M: Wow, that's cool.

L: So, do you think I could go to Niihau one day?

M: I don't know. It's not so easy. I mean there are only a few trips every year.

L: But you were able to do it ...

M: That's right but I don't think I could have done it on my own. My parents paid for me to go there. It was very expensive.

L: I can imagine. Wow. I cannot believe that you got to visit your very own desert island.

M: Me neither. Feels like a bit of a dream now, but it was the most amazing experience of my life.

▶ 36 page 46 exercises A and B

N = News anchor, C = Correspondent

N: OK, next up on the show we have a bizarre true crime story from the Florida area. Our Miami correspondent Clarence Miller is here to tell us all about it. Clarence.

C: Well, Amy, this is really an incredible story. You're going find it very hard to believe! Last week a Florida man, Bradley Philips, was arrested for burglary after calling the police.

N: Back up a minute. The guy was the burglar, and he called the police?

C: That's right.

N: Whoa! How did that happen? Did he have a fight with his partner?

C: No, he committed the crime alone. What happened was that, while Philips was burgling the Miami address, he dropped his cellphone.

N: You mean he left his phone behind in the house?

C: Exactly. The police arrived at the house to investigate the burglary. Suddenly, they heard a phone ringing. They looked around until they found a cellphone on the bed.

N: Did the officers answer the call?

C: You bet they did! They asked who was calling and Philips gave them his address and asked the police to return his phone.

N: So the police went to his house, grabbed him and Philips confessed to his crime?

C: Not at all. When the police accused Philips of burglary, he denied it. Absolutely. He insisted that his phone had been stolen.

N: Was he telling the truth?

C: Absolutely not. He totally made the story up. What gave him away was the fact that the owner of the house had seen him leaving the property.

N: So someone saw him do it?

C: That's right and what's more, the police took fingerprints from his phone and linked those prints to five more burglaries in the area.

N: So then did he own up?

C: No! When Philips went to court, he kept on lying. He still said his phone had been stolen and he denied that anyone saw him near the scene of the burglary.

N: That is astonishing.

C: You're telling me. The crime of the century it was not.

▶ 39 page 48 exercises C and D

D = Dave, S = Sharon

D: That's just awful. Well, my worst travel experience ever was a flight last year from Japan to France.

S: Yeah? What happened?

D: The man in the seat next to me had a very red face and he was sweating a lot. I mean, his shirt was wet. It turned out that he was having a heart attack.

S: Oh, my goodness. And you're a doctor!

D: Yes. I happened to be in the right place at the right time. He was Japanese and he didn't speak much English so I just diagnosed what was happening. So I started performing first

aid when the co-pilot came to speak to me. He said in a loud voice "Do you want me to make an emergency landing?" Everybody on the plane looked at me in silence. For whatever reason, the man said "no, no", and he held my hand, so I thought he was not in immediate danger. As luck would have it, we were very near our final destination so I said we should carry on.

S: What a responsibility.

D: In the end, we arrived in Paris and an ambulance team came on the plane. The local doctor was French but strangely enough she spoke Japanese and she took control of the situation.

S: Astonishing.

D: Yeah. Anyway, in the end, the passenger survived, though he hasn't been allowed to travel again. I think he's in a wheelchair now.

S: Does he communicate with you?

D: Not regularly, but he did send me a beautiful thank you letter. And, the airline gave me two free first-class tickets to go anywhere in the world to say thank you.

S: I think you deserved them!

▶ 44 page 53 exercises A and B

1 Baseball. Paulo Orlando has made headlines around the world as he becomes the first Brazilian ever to play in the World Series. Lining up for the Kansas City Royals, it's been a double celebration for the São Paolo born player as his team brought home the trophy, defeating the New York Mets four games to one.

2 This has to be the weirdest job around, but it really happens. Families are paid to live in empty homes. The family moves in and lives in the house as normal, but they have to keep it clean. It turns out that house buyers are more inclined to buy a property if it feels like a home, so companies pay people to live in them. However, whenever a potential buyer comes around, the family has to be out. Worst of all, when someone buys the house, the family has to leave and find another empty house to call home.

3 It's the world's biggest burger and it's made right here in Southgate Michigan. Yes, we are home to Mallie's Sports Bar and Grill, where they make the largest burger in the world. We ordered one to check it out, but be warned: the burger weighs around 150 kilos and you have to order it 72 hours in advance. Don't use the drive-thru because you'll never get it in your car.

4 Russia's legendary Bolshoi Ballet has toured the United States many times, but this year the company has announced its first ever visit to Canada. Dance fans will be able to see *Swan Lake* in Toronto, followed by five performances of *Don Quixote* in Ottawa. It promises to be a once-in-a lifetime opportunity for Canadians to see the world's premier dance company locally.

5 Professor Kieran Mullen of Oklahoma University became so tired of his students failing to pay attention in class that he decided to take drastic action. Taking a laptop computer, he placed it in liquid

65

Selected audio scripts

nitrogen. At that point, the computer was still OK. The physics professor proceeded to drop the machine on the floor where it broke into hundreds of pieces. The students were stunned, but it was a hoax – Mullen had planted a broken laptop at the front of the class to use in his "experiment".

▶ 48 *page 58 exercises A and B*

K = Keith Woods, J = Jenna Doyle

K: Hello, I'm Keith Woods.

J: And I'm Jenna Doyle. Today on the podcast, we discuss how a little bit of pessimism can actually be good for you. Keith, would you like to start off?

K: Sure. We'd all love to look on the bright side and think positively about our lives. On the other hand, we view pessimism as bad, a destructive pattern of behavior. Actually, it's turns out it's good to have a bit of both.

J: Absolutely, especially when we're talking about money. It can be a financial risk to be an optimist. Believing that things will always get better encourages people to borrow. Optimists always believe they'll be able to pay it back, which is not always the case.

K: No. It's not always wise to hope for the best.

J: There are also studies that suggest that pessimistic people are more effective in the workplace.

K: Which is strange, because you have to be positive and smiley on job interviews.

J: Interviews are one thing, but real work is another. Because pessimists can predict many different problems in the future, they make better plans than optimists. Hoping that nothing bad will happen in the future is just wishful thinking.

K: True. Now one thing that surprised me is that pessimism also has some health advantages.

J: Is that really true?

K: It seems so. German doctors discovered that pessimists are 10% more likely to have better health in the future than optimists.

J: Why?

K: It's possibly because pessimists panic about health problems and seek medical attention early on. When it comes to your health, the "no news is good news" strategy is not always the best. Optimists sometimes ignore a medical problem until it's too late to solve it.

J: I see.

K: Being optimistic can be dangerous to your health in other ways. Optimists don't believe that bad things will happen to them, so they don't take basic safety precautions like wearing a helmet when riding a bike. More people are seriously injured in bike accidents because they don't have appropriate protection. Better safe than sorry.

J: So, next time someone complains that being a pessimist is "toxic", remember there are benefits to looking on the bad side of life.

Answer key

Unit 1

1.1

A 1 mother-in-law 2 step daughter
3 great grandfather/granddad
4 only child 5 twins 6 brother/cousin

B 1 single 2 stepfather/stepdad
3 half-brother 4 only 5 father-in-law

C 1 made up 2 runs in 3 get along
4 look up 5 look after

D Students' own answers

1.2

A Students' own answers

B 1 become 2 understand 3 have an
opportunity 4 arrive at 5 received
6 becomes

C 1 Not asking for help is a bad idea.
2 It started raining, but we carried on
playing tennis.
3 It's not worth going to the exhibit on
Sunday.
4 Having a new baby is totally exhausting.
5 I can't help feeling nervous about next
week's exams.
6 I have a hard time thinking of new ideas
for work.

D Students' own answers

1.3

A 2

B 1 b 2 e 3 a

C 1 ownership 2 affectionate
3 neighborhood 4 helpful 5 freedom
6 talkative 7 careless 8 happiness

D Students' own answers

1.4

A 1 family doesn't want to pay for the wedding
2 brother hasn't taken care of the
invitations yet
3 cousin can't come to the wedding
4 aunt is calling him a lot

B 1 T 2 F 3 F 4 F 5 T 6 F

C 1 It's essential for you to tell
2 It's better not to give
3 It's advisable to send
4 It's hard not to get
5 It's a good idea for you to ask
6 There's no point choosing

D Students' own answers

1.5

A 1 it's important 2 To begin with
3 On top of that 4 Besides 5 Lastly

B 1 c 2 b 3 a

C Students' own answers

D 1 family words 2 being young 3 pets,
like a dog 4 the grammar: *hard to*
(adjective + infinitive) 5 making voice
calls

E Students' own answers

Unit 2

2.1

A Across: 1 clock 4 issues 5 crash
6 brain 7 patterns
Down: 2 leisure 3 dinner 4 instant
7 peer

B 1 romantic relationships 2 Financial
problems 3 material possessions
4 Physical appearance 5 scientific fact

C 1 ~~worry~~ worrying 2 think ~~to~~ about
3 ~~making~~ to make 4 ~~to think~~ thinking
5 ~~consider~~ 'm considering

D Students' own answers

2.2

A 1 wears off 2 weight gain 3 treat
4 at a disadvantage 5 a big deal
6 keep you going

B 1 with 2 thing 3 of 4 eating 5 is

C 1 that 2 worst 3 it can place 4 that
5 These are 6 of 7 are 8 being
9 keeping 10 with

2.3

A The author believes it's more important to
look intelligent.

B 1 of 2 at 3 to 4 at 5 at 6 for

C 3 and 5

D 1 second 2 its 3 which 4 them
5 one 6 whose

2.4

A Doesn't believe it exists: Frank Mortimer,
Alba Lopez
Thinks it might exist: Rachel Schultz

B 1 ~~goats~~ sheep 2 ~~brown~~ red
3 ~~Argentina~~ Mexico 4 ~~tired~~ thin

C 1 must 2 might just want 3 have been
4 may exist

D 1 have seen 2 have been 3 have left
4 have made 5 have rained

2.5

A 1 while 2 One advantage of 3 A further
advantage 4 a number of drawbacks
5 On the one hand 6 On the other hand
7 To sum up

B 1 F 2 F 3 A 4 A

C Students' own answers

D 1 thinking about things, what's on your
mind 2 food, eating out 3 ways to learn
and be intelligent 4 spaceships, UFOs and
science fiction 5 being a genius, having a
high IQ

E Students' own answers

Unit 3

3.1

A 1 yawn 2 push 3 trip 4 stare 5 pull
6 glance 7 scream 8 picture a

B 1 pushed 2 yawned 3 glanced
4 screamed 5 whispered

C 1 go 2 happens 3 know 4 then
5 believe 6 thing

3.2

A 1 was traveling 2 took 3 was working
4 captured 5 had been waiting
6 appeared 7 arrived 8 hit 9 had put
10 went

B 1 was walking 2 dropped 3 had been
taking / had taken 4 were camping
5 had left 6 was watching

C Students' own answers

3.3

A The author likes it: the toasting knife
The author doesn't like it: PEG
The author gives no opinion: ice cream

B 1 slice 2 vegans 3 it's up to me
4 pricey 5 stick 6 handy 7 pops up
8 glow-in-the-dark

C 1 downs 2 cons 3 soul 4 worse
5 face 6 over

3.4

A 1 Mary 2 Ron 3 Ron 4 Mary
5 Mary 6 Ron

B 1 F 2 T 3 F 4 T 5 F 6 F

C 1 my mom bought me a surfboard
2 We won the State Championship
3 I used to collect / I would collect
4 I didn't use to have any hobbies

D Students' own answers

3.5

A 1 as 2 Initially 3 Some time later
4 in the meantime 5 Eventually
6 All of a sudden 7 Finally

B 1 Initially 2 while 3 In the meantime
4 Finally 5 suddenly 6 After a while

C 1 ~~suddenly~~ sudden 2 ~~late~~ later
3 ~~meanwhile~~ meantime 4 it initially
5 after a while

D 1 ways of looking: *stare, glance* 2 selfies
3 binomials: *safe and sound*
4 the grammar: *used to*
5 happiness and feeling happy

E Students' own answers

Unit 4

4.1

A 1 out 2 in 3 out 4 for 5 out
6 away 7 apart

B 1 Surely you'll agree that
2 doesn't mean it's authentic
3 Look at it this way.
4 You're missing the point!
5 Let me put it another way.

C Students' own answers

4.2

A 1 F 2 F 3 T

B 1 Even though 2 Unlike 3 whereas
4 In spite 5 Despite

C 1 c 2 f 3 a 4 e 5 b

D Students' own answers

67

Answer key

4.3

A 1 d 2 f 3 a 4 c 5 e

B 1 In the end 2 At first 3 Back in the day
4 at some point 5 From time to time
6 in no time

C 1 wildfire 2 cats and dogs 3 the wind
4 a broken record 5 a glove 6 a bird

4.4

A 1 T 2 F 3 T

B 1 b 2 c 3 c 4 a 5 b

C 1 by 2 each 3 another 4 ourselves
5 yourself

D 1 each 2 himself 3 another 4 myself
5 ourselves 6 yourself 7 other
8 ourselves 9 another 10 herself

4.5

A 5 stars

B a 4 b 2 c 5 d 1 e 6 f 3

C 1 for the most part 2 average
3 Generally speaking 4 By and large
5 on the whole 6 As a rule 7 Overall

D Students' own answers

E 1 being deceived by appearances
2 the potential end of schooling
3 hearing gossip spread by others "through
the grapevine" 4 the grammar: *each other*
5 the expression *dying for* (in the song line is
used literally, not figuratively)

F Students' own answers

Unit 5

5.1

A a 3 b 2 d 4 e 1

B 1 b 2 c 3 b 4 a 5 c

C 1 1969 2 5th 3 10 4 2003 5 42

D 1 wish 2 destruction 3 a lot of money
4 luck at

5.2

A 1 lived 2 had 3 had never moved
4 had been 5 knew 6 hadn't lost

B 1 ~~can~~ could 2 ~~would~~ wouldn't 3 ~~didn't drop~~ hadn't dropped 4 ~~have~~ had 5 ~~had replied~~ replied 6 ~~does~~ did

C 1 Do 2 at 3 get 4 with 5 You'll

D Students' own answers

5.3

A 1 international 2 underestimate
3 overworked 4 underqualified
5 underachievers 6 overestimate
7 underprivileged 8 underpaid

B 1 underpaid 2 oversimplify
3 underrated 4 overachievers
5 overacting 6 underestimated

C 1 hardly ~~no~~ any 2 ~~interested~~ interesting
3 ~~none~~ no 4 ~~nothing~~ anything

5.4

A Intended: 1, 2, 5 Did: 3, 4

B 1 F 2 F 3 T 4 F 5 T 6 F

C 1 hadn't been 2 had chosen 3 would
live / would be living 4 wouldn't have
found 5 would have driven / would
drive 6 wouldn't be working

D Students' own answers

5.5

A 1 b 2 d 3 a 4 c 5 e

B 1 tranquil 2 devastating 3 shocked
4 exhausted 5 huge 6 terrified
7 amazing 8 legendary

C Students' own answers

D 1 being someone's hero 2 the grammar:
wishing, an imaginary situation
3 dropping out of college and not getting a
degree 4 regretting a mistake, wishing to
go back to yesterday and retract it 5 not
being very lucky (because he wasn't born
into a powerful family)

E Students' own answers

Unit 6

6.1

A 1 teachers 2 bag 3 the password
4 Flight attendants

B Topic 3 1 Google 2 Bing
3 DuckDuckGo 4 CCSearch

C 1 Google 2 DuckDuckGo 3 Bing
4 CCSearch

D 1 and 4

E risk is not, that is changing, that is
guaranteed, is not taking

6.2

A 1 A video from my YouTube account
has been taken and used without my
permission.
2 I had my blog hacked so when people
looked at it, they saw an ad for second-
hand cell phones.
3 You would be shocked if you Googled
yourself.
4 Lots of photos of me have been put on
Facebook by my friends.
5 A rumor about you is being spread on
Twitter (by a group of people).
6 A programmer was asked by Nick to
design his website for him.

B 1 believe it or not. 2 Here's the thing.
3 I don't see it that way. 4 point taken
5 what's your take on it 6 couldn't agree
more

C 1 I totally agree. 2 That makes sense.
3 Listen to what I'm about to say.
4 Look, here's the thing. 5 Point taken.

D Students' own answers

6.3

A 2

B 1 his blog 2 these dangers 3 people
(who take control of the camera)
4 a password 5 a blue light 6 covering
the webcam

C 1, 2 and 5

D Students' own answers

6.4

A 2

B 1 Whenever 2 whoever 3 However
4 Whichever 5 Whatever

C 1 b 2 f 3 d 4 a 5 c

D Students' own answers

6.5

A Students' own answers

B 1 As far as possible 2 Never ever
3 Whatever you do 4 Avoid using
5 be sure to use 6 Do your best

C A 5 B 3 C 7 D 1 E 6 F 4

D Students' own answers

E 1 offering somebody protection 2 privacy,
not being able to contact someone 3 being
spied upon 4 the grammar: question
words with -ever 5 keeping (or not
keeping) secrets

F Students' own answers

Unit 7

7.1

A 1 regarded 2 rose 3 released 4 came
5 high-profile 6 took

B 1 had 2 get 3 of 4 got 5 on 6 into

C Students' own answers

7.2

A 1 h 2 c 3 a 4 d 5 f 6 b

B 1 ~~so that~~ 2 ~~Because of~~ 3 ~~due to~~
4 ~~since~~ 5 ~~in order to~~ 6 As

C 1 ~~so~~ because 2 in order **to** beat 3 correct
4 ~~for~~ to 5 ~~So that~~ Because / As

7.3

A 1 F 2 T

B 1 e 2 c 3 b 4 a 5 d

C 1 profit 2 dud 3 guaranteed 4 melted
5 overseas

D 1 caught on 2 lacked 3 didn't live up to
4 backfired 5 failed to

7.4

A 1 d 2 a 3 b 4 c

B 1 F 2 F 3 F 4 T 5 T 6 T 7 T 8 F

C 1 ~~students~~ student 2 ~~was~~ were
3 ~~others~~ other 4 ~~other~~ another
5 ~~other~~ others 6 ~~other~~ 7 correct
8 ~~others~~ other

7.5

A 1 incredibly 2 occasionally
3 surprisingly 4 easily 5 disappointingly
6 hugely 7 consistently 8 cleverly
9 absolutely 10 firmly

B 1 C 2 D 3 not answered 4 B 5 E
6 A

C Students' own answers

D 1 Adele's in the quiz and these lines are
from one of her songs. 2 It's a line from
Party in the USA, Miley's first worldwide
hit. 3 The word *rebel* is both a noun and a
verb, in which the stress changes.
4 analysing pictures 5 the adverb
modifying the verb: *seeing clearly*

E Students' own answers

Unit 8

8.1

A 1 I'm terrified of flying. 2 Prawns freak me out. 3 Unlike many people, snakes don't bother me. 4 I don't mind dogs at all. 5 I avoid giving presentations on my job. 6 Spiders make me a bit uneasy.

B 1 heart 2 passed 3 tears 4 sweat 5 stomach 6 dizzy 7 breathe

C Students' own answers

8.2

A 1 M 2 L 3 L 4 M 5 L 6 M

B 1 ~~unpleasant~~ difficult 2 ~~worked~~ lived 3 ~~boat~~ helicopter 4 ~~No one~~ Everyone 5 ~~golden~~ white 6 ~~month~~ year 7 ~~company~~ parents 8 ~~terrifying~~ amazing

C 1 couldn't 2 was able to 3 could / were able to 4 was able to 5 couldn't / weren't able to

D Students' own answers

8.3

A 1 cope with 2 spread 3 carried out 4 boosting 5 spread 6 undergoing

B A 3 B 4 C 1 D 6 E 2

C 1 popularity 2 confidence 3 promise 4 changes 5 lies 6 demands
Gray adjective: afraid

8.4

A 1 d 2 c 3 a 4 e

B 1 can't / aren't allowed to 2 ✓ 3 ✓ 4 can't / aren't allowed to 5 shouldn't 6 are allowed to park

C 1 'd better 2 don't have to 3 aren't supposed to 4 ought to 5 're allowed to

D Students' own answers

8.5

A 1, 2, 3, 5, 6 and 7

B 1 mean 2 For starters 3 so to speak 4 That said 5 Trust 6 Other than that 7 Needless to say 8 Thank goodness

C talking about your fears can help you cope, breathing exercises, do some exercise, don't drink caffeinated drinks, get plenty of rest
Students' own answers

D 1 being paralyzed by fear 2 the grammar: using couldn't to express inability in the past 3 living surrounded by fear and fear-mongering 4 the grammar: supposed to 5 dealing with and getting over problems

E Students' own answers

Unit 9

9.1

A 1 mingle 2 keep quiet 3 small talk 4 reveal 5 thinking out loud

B 1 We're in the process of thinking it over.
2 I showed the invitation to him by mistake.
3 Yeah, we sent them a present last week.
4 My mom thought it up.
5 I'll send them an email right away.
6 The caterers prepared the food absolutely beautifully.

C Students' own answers

9.2

A Students' own answers

B A 3 B 6 C 1 D 4 E 2 F 5

C 1 that 2 it 3 it 4 which 5 where 6 it

D Students' own answers

9.3

A 1

B 1 C 2 E 3 A 4 F 5 B 6 D

C 1 value 2 outlook 3 less 4 tolerant 5 under 6 to 7 aware

D Students' own answers

9.4

A 1 e 2 c 3 b 4 d 5 a

B ~~an apartment~~ a house, ~~robbery~~ burglary, ~~on a sofa~~ on a bed, ~~his brother~~ the burglar, ~~name~~ address, ~~lost~~ stolen, ~~messages~~ fingerprints, ~~four~~ five

C 1 ~~who was~~ 2 ~~who are~~ 3 ~~who was~~ 4 ~~who requires~~ requiring 5 ~~which are~~ 6 ~~that has been~~ 7 ~~arrive~~ arriving

D 1 arrest 2 suspect 3 deny 4 nod 5 comment 6 allow

9.5

A 1 as 2 Unlike 3 in order to 4 despite 5 Due to 6 so that 7 While 8 because 9 Although

B 1 T 2 F 3 F 4 F 5 T

C 1 ~~Not like~~ Unlike 2 ~~have~~ having 3 ~~studying~~ study 4 ~~what~~ that 5 ~~it was~~ the 6 because ~~of~~

D 1 needing to spend time alone, on our own 2 rudeness 3 different generations 4 catching people who lie 5 anti-consumerism; money isn't everything

E Students' own answers

Unit 10

10.1

A 1 looking forward to 2 got through 3 get away 4 dawned on 5 end up 6 mixed up

B 1 ~~go~~ going 2 dawned **on** me 3 got through it 4 correct 5 mixing us up

C 1 doctor 2 Japan 3 France 4 (Japanese) man / passenger 5 two free first-class 6 anywhere

D 1 F 2 F 3 F 4 T 5 T 6 F

E Students' own answers

10.2

A 1 mix-up 2 rip-off 3 breakdown 4 login 5 checkout

B 1 they are 2 it takes 3 to know 4 whether 5 it is open 6 I get

C 1 I'd like to know whether summer in your country is very hot. / summer is very hot in your country.
2 Could you tell me what time most stores open in your capital city?
3 Do you happen to know the name of a good restaurant near your home?

D Students' own answers

10.3

A clothes, meals, the cost of living, useful phrases, people's homes, the character of the people

B 1 F 2 T 3 F 4 F 5 T 6 F

C 1 F 2 L 3 L 4 F 5 L 6 F

D Students' own answers

10.4

A 1 hustle and bustle 2 homesick 3 overwhelming 4 culture clash 5 let alone 6 barely

B 1 was 2 I'm 3 gotten 4 are already 5 get 6 I'm 7 cannot get

C 1 slowly **getting** used 2 ~~got~~ get 3 correct 4 ~~be~~ get 5 ~~use~~ used 6 ~~get~~ am

10.5

A 1 blew 2 set 3 stunning 4 gorgeous 5 awe-inspiring 6 take 7 beyond

B a 3 b 5 c 1 d 6 e 4 f 2

C Students' own answers

D 1 traveling 2 the grammar: indirect questions 3 going home, making a home somewhere 4 the grammar: be used to 5 a report on a city

E Students' own answers

Unit 11

11.1

A 1 Sports 2 Property 3 Eating out 4 Arts 5 Education

B 1 ~~Argentinian~~ Brazilian, ~~lost~~ won 2 ~~don't~~ have to clean, must ~~always~~ **never** be at home 3 ~~Northgate~~ Southgate, ~~the day~~ 72 hours 4 ~~are frequent visitors~~ have never previously visited, ~~Nutcracker~~ Swan Lake 5 ~~oxygen~~ nitrogen, ~~two pieces~~ hundreds of pieces

C 1 biased 2 behind-the-scenes 3 an accurate source 4 keep up with 5 caught my eye 6 skip

D Students' own answers

11.2

A 1 lost 2 freaked 3 cool 4 calm 5 together

B 1 Rodrigo said there were some strangers in our apartment.
2 Rodrigo said no flights had been able to leave that day because of the volcano.
3 The mother said they had booked the apartment online.
4 The father said they could always stay at a hotel.
5 Rodrigo said he'd never forgive me for that.
6 I told Rodrigo I was really, really sorry.

C 1 Rodrigo asked the family what they were doing there.
2 Rodrigo asked when I was coming back.
3 The mother asked whether there had been a mistake.
4 We asked the family where they would go.

69

Answer key

11.3

A 1 C 2 D 3 A 4 E 5 B
B 1 NI 2 T 3 F 4 F 5 T 6 F
C 1 d 2 c 3 b 4 f 5 e 6 a

11.4

A 1 didn't tell a soul 2 My lips are sealed.
3 spread it around 4 have my word
5 keep it to yourself 6 Me and my big
mouth. 7 between you and me 8 never
guess

B 1 urged me **to** do 2 ~~no~~ not 3 **to** help me
4 me **to** go to 5 ~~throwing~~ to throw
6 correct 7 refused **to** refund
8 ~~to~~ change

C 1 to repeat 2 not to tell 3 to join
4 to play 5 take part 6 to hear

11.5

A 1, 3, 4 and 5
B 1 regard 2 belief 3 matters 4 reality
5 call
C Students' own answers
D 1 a news story 2 the grammar: a reported
statement 3 The Rebecca Black song
from ex 7A in the lesson 4 the grammar:
reporting what people say 5 fame and
dealing with being famous
E Students' own answers

Unit 12

12.1

A 1 A 2 D 3 A 4 D 5 A
B 1 behavior 2 borrow 3 job interviews
4 plans 5 German 6 ignore 7 safety
8 toxic / bad
C 1 dream 2 good 3 wishful 4 safe
5 best 6 bright

12.2

A 1 be making 2 have completely finished
3 have already recognized 4 work 5 sit
6 will need 7 will be working
8 continue 9 be using
10 is going to save

B 1 We'll have finished our project by
March 4th.
2 The population is bound to keep growing.
3 This time tomorrow, we'll be sitting on a
beach in Acapulco.
4 Everyone will have left before/by
midnight, I promise you.
5 In 2050, people are going to be living on
the surface of Mars.
6 Barcelona FC is likely to win the league
next year.

C 1 by Shakespeare 2 made by 3 by taxi,
by midnight 4 by 10%, by even more

12.3

A 1 north-western Russia 2 –71 Centigrade
3 the water that doesn't freeze 4 when the
temperature falls below –50 Centigrade
5 two days

B 2, 3 and 5

C 1 have, doubts 2 pulled, off 3 figure out
4 have, clue 5 pose, threat

12.4

A 1 It always leaves, it comes back
2 I'll watch 3 I'll help 4 it's going to
rain 5 I'm not doing 6 will win

B 1 are we meeting / are we going to meet
2 're coming / 're going to come 3 'm
going to write 4 's bringing / 's going to
bring 5 'll call 6 'm going to stay / 'm
staying 7 'll come 8 'll go 9 'll feel

C 1 ~~will arrive~~ arrives 2 ~~I'll leave~~ I leave
3 correct 4 ~~will meet~~ meet 5 ~~tell~~ will
tell 6 ~~I'll get paid~~ I get

D Students' own answers

12.5

A 1 Hopefully 2 finally 3 definitely
4 certainly 5 officially 6 inevitably
7 eventually 8 probably

B 1 when the email was written 2 use it
as an opportunity to travel 3 English
is important for your career 4 further
practice after the course 5 look on the
bright side

C Students' own answers

D 1 the problems of being an optimist
2 what will and won't disappear in
the future 3 the grammar: *bound to*
4 trying to make an excuse, but not doing it
very well 5 imagining the future

E Students' own answers